Jesus Reveals Revelation

Acknowledgements

I would like to acknowledge Dr. Stephen Breck Reid, Academic Dean and Professor of Old Testament, Bethany Theological Seminary for his encouragement, guidance, and thoughtful insights in writhing this book, and Dr. Karen Lebacqz for introducing us. Dr. Reid taught me that you learn from your heart as well as your mind and for that I am most grateful.

I also thank Susan Flowers Walker for her encouragement and support.

And, most important of all, I thank our Lord Jesus Christ for the inspiration.

About the Author: Charles Huettner

The book of Revelation intrigued Charles from his teenage years. He yearned to fully understand what the revelation truly means. In December 2002, he got the idea that God's direction to Jesus to tell believers what will happen might be true on two levels; one through showing John what to write in Revelation, and the other showing believers how to interpret it from Jesus' words in other parts of the Bible. Charles began assembling related verses to see if they would provide an answer, and they did. The result is this book "Jesus Reveals Revelation".

Like Jesus' followers during his days on earth, Charles has been drawn into the ministry from another profession. He is the President of Charles Huettner Associates LLC, an aerospace consulting firm. In addition, he is the Executive Director of the Aerospace States Association (ASA) that is comprised of Lt. Governors and delegates from the nation's 50 states focusing on aerospace related education and economic development issues. Charles has a talent for understanding the "Big Picture". He has had the opportunity to use that talent in his professional career and his Bible study.

Charles retired after 33 years of government service as the Executive Director of the Presidential "Commission on the Future of the U.S. Aerospace Industry". Prior to this, he was the Senior Policy Advisor for Aviation for the National Science and Technology Council (NSTC), in the Executive Office of the President under the Clinton and G.W. Bush Administrations. He was also the Director for Aviation Safety Research at NASA. At FAA, he rose through the ranks from inspector to serve as Deputy Associate Administrator for Aviation Safety. In 2005, he published the National Institute of Aerospace report "Responding to the Call: Aviation Plan for American Leadership.

Charles is an Airline Transport Pilot rated in the B-747, B- 727 and the Air Force C-141 Starlifter. He retired as a Colonel in the USAF Reserves where he last served as the Reserve Augmentee to the Air Force Chief of Safety. His decorations include the Legion of Merit, Meritorious Service Medal, the Air Medal, the Air Force Commendation Medal, the Armed Forces Expeditionary Medal, the Combat Readiness Medal, and the Vietnam Service Medal.

Charles has a BS Degree in Industrial Management from the University of Akron and a Masters Degree in Public Administration from Harvard's John F. Kennedy School of Government. He has a Diploma in Theological Studies from the Virginia Theological Seminary.

Jesus Reveals Revelation

BY CHARLES HUETTNER

Jesus Reveals Revelation

Table of Contents

Introduction

For over 40 years I have studied the Bible and wondered about the book of Revelation and what it really means. As I studied and prayed a thought came to me; perhaps Jesus has provided the information in the Bible that would unlock the mysteries of Revelation. I believe that He has.

This book is a thoughtful guide to understanding Revelation based on Jesus' interpretation, and insights that came to me on my devotional journey as I wrote this book.

To take you on my journey, I bring verses together from across the Bible that relate to the verses in Revelation. I insert my discussion of why I have organized the verses in this way and provide you with my insights so that you can see the logic and inspiration for yourself. To do this without confusing you in the process, I developed a methodology that uses italics, fonts, and underlining to keep your oriented.

Here is the methodology I used in writing this book.

1. My discussion and comments relating to the scripture are in italics and the verses from the Bible are not. In this way you will know if the thoughts come from me or from God.
2. I have retained the original Biblical references so that you can see where each verse comes from.
3. I use fonts to distinguish between Revelation, Old and New Testament verses. Verses from Revelation are black Arial type, the Old Testament is indented and in Courier, and New Testament is indented in Times New Roman type. In this way Old and New Testament verses that are pertinent to a given section in Revelation can be pulled together in order to present a Bible-wide view of what is being said. My hope is that the indentation and

change in font will help you to remain oriented when I bring other parts of the Bible into the discussion of Revelation. (The fonts cannot be changed in some EBooks, but the verses are indented.)

4. I have underlined words in the biblical text that are pertinent to my discussion of insights, and annotated in bold, words that I want to highlight throughout the scripture.

5. Many of the verses in the Gospels that talk of the end-time leap forward at the end of the discussion to the end of Revelation, but the initial focus is on an earlier time in the end time chronology. I will point this out in my discussion of the text.

6. When the gospel quotes Jesus saying "My name" he is saying what we now call "Christians".

7. One of the keys to understanding Revelation is focusing on the words used. For the purpose of our discussion, I need to define the meaning of the word "words". In Revelation, it says not to add or take away from the words in the revelation yet the words were written originally for the most part in Hebrew or Greek. These words were then translated into English (and other languages) by different groups of scholars who have selected different specific words that they believe most accurately capture the meaning of the original text in the new language. So when we talk of words we actually mean the underlying meaning of the original words. I have used one Bible translation for consistency in this book, the New American Standard version of the Bible. If you look at the specific words in other translations of the Bible some will be slightly different, but the meaning of the words remains essentially the same.

8. I do not add or delete any word from the Revelation text.

9. Appendix A contains numerous definitions of words used in Revelation that are defined in the Bible itself. I will discuss these as they occur in this book.

10. Appendix B contains the complete reordered Revelation for you to read without my comments or highlighting. I hope that you will use this as a reference for further study on your own.

I will now take you on a devotional journey into Revelation. I pray that your journey will be as insightful as my own. I also hope that you will use this book as part of your church Bible study. It is sure to result in "Spirited" discussion.

Chapter 1. Keys to Unlocking Revelation

Jesus' Challenges

Seven-headed beasts, plagues, fire and brimstone, Armageddon, God's triumph over Satan; this is the picture that many people have of the book of Revelation. But, while much has been written about Revelation, people have struggled for nearly 2000 years to understand this last book in the Bible. This was certainly the case for me. I believed that Revelation describes what will happen in the future; the glorious return of Christ, the fate of this world, and the beginning of the next. But, the story is so filled with symbolism and is so hard to understand that, for a long time, I believed that Revelation is something that simply must be taken on faith. And yet, Revelation begins with the charge that it is a message to show Jesus' followers "the things that must shortly take place". This clearly says that we need to understand the revelation message, yet it seems unclear. Why would God send us a message that we could not understand and then expect us to follow it? How could I understand the truth? This was the first challenge of Revelation to me.

A second challenge comes from Matthew 24:4. Jesus said, "See that no one misleads you". An example of how I might be misled comes from the very next verse in Matthew 24:5; "For many will come in My name, saying, 'I am the Christ' and will mislead many." This verse can be interpreted two ways. One can read verse 5 to say that many will come in Christ's name claiming to be the Christ, or read it to say that many will come in Christ's name (acknowledging that He is the Christ) and will mislead many. The first interpretation leads you to believe that many false Christs will arise, where the second means that people who acknowledge Christ as Lord will do the misleading. In other words, believers could mislead other believers without even knowing it. Therefore, it is not unexpected that people will interpret portions of the Bible in different ways. So whose interpretation should I believe and follow? And, if I become so certain of a particular interpretation could I be misled and set up for a fall when the end-times come.

The bottom line, Jesus challenged me to try to understand the book of Revelation and to not be misled. As I studied and prayed for a way to address these challenges a thought came to me; could it be that Jesus has left us the information we need to unlock the mystery of the book of Revelation elsewhere in the Bible? This began my effort to assemble all the verses in the Bible that address the end-times and, through the wonders of word processing, insert them into the book of Revelation where they appeared to fit. As I began to bring similar subjects from across the Bible together, I realized that Jesus told us the order of end-time events in the Gospels. This is what started me on the journey to write this book. Once begun, my spine tingled as each chapter finally fell into place. It is an amazing story that is different than what I expected when I began. Jesus has provided us what we need to unlock Revelation.

I have experienced a spiritual transformation by my interaction with the Bible while writing this book and I think you will too by reading it. If you have struggled with the book of Revelation let me be your guide. I will show you the keys that will transform Revelation into an easily understood message from God. I discovered these keys through a devotional journey to understand Revelation based on Jesus' words in the Bible. I will take you along on my journey and share with you the understanding that Jesus' words opened up to me. But first, let me introduce myself.

The Keys

As you can see from my biographical summary in the front of this book, I have spent my professional career in aviation and aerospace. So, why is a pilot and government executive writing a book about Revelation? That story goes back to a trip home from high school in 1961 when Jesus through the Holy Spirit first touched me. I have now retired from the government having completed a most amazing career in aviation. It stated with flying as a C-141 transport pilot to Viet Nam and around the world, and ended as Senior Policy Advisor for Aviation at the White House. I use the term amazing not only because of the career opportunities I have had, but also because of how the Spirit has worked in my life along the way. Major obstacles in my career turned into opportunities and "coincidences" became key events in the achievement of policy issues I was involved with. I believe with certainty that the Holy Spirit is actively involved in my life and has led me to see into the mysteries of his book of Revelation while writing this book for you.

Writing this book was a devotional journey for me. As I progressed from rewrite to rewrite new insights emerged. I realized that understanding Revelation is vital for everyone living today. It is God's message to all mankind to tell us what will happen. It is, therefore, the only way to understand what is really happening in the world and to prepare ourselves for what we will face. I discovered that Revelation also answers many of the questions that have troubled mankind over the centuries such as; why are we born, why God lets good people suffer, what happens when we die, where is heaven, and others. So where to begin?

There have been uncountable numbers of interpretations of Revelation since it was written and there is no way to definitively prove any of them. That is what led me to see what Jesus had to say. Most Biblical scholars do not believe that Revelation is a prophecy. They have studied first century Christian churches as best as they can, and the Roman Empire that were the rulers at the time Revelation was written. They conclude that Revelation is a coded message from John to the seven churches. In most scholars' view, John, not the apostle, was writing to the churches of his day to tell them to keep the faith during the terrible tribulations of the Roman Emperor Nero and his immediate successor's reigns. Scholars believe that John wrote to the churches using symbology from the Old Testament (OT) prophets. In this way, John could send the churches encouragement in terms that early church members were familiar with from reading OT scripture. It is thought that John believed that the Romans would not understand his letter so it would not add justification to their persecution of the churches.

However, my spirit would not rest with the answers of scholars. To begin, some scholars and I do believe that it was the Apostle John that wrote Revelation. John was the disciple who Jesus loved and was not captured and killed during Nero's attack on Christians, as were Peter and Paul. In addition, I believe that John's Gospel gives us a clue to the fact that he lived longer than expected to complete the work that Christ had for him to do.

> John 21:21-23 (NASB)
> 21 So Peter seeing him said to Jesus, "Lord, and what about this man?"
> 22 Jesus said to him, "If **I want him to remain until I come,** what is that to you? You follow Me!"
> 23 Therefore this saying went out among the brethren that that disciple would not die; yet Jesus did not say to him that he would not die, but only, "If I want him to remain until I come, what is that to you?"

I believe that John did remain until Christ came. He lived to see Christ come in the revelation that Christ showed His friend the

Apostle John. John lived long enough to write the story of Christ's second coming for us.

While John certainly wrote to encourage the people of his day, I believe God was also speaking to another generation. Revelation has two messages; one that John was writing to his generation and those that followed, and a second that God made sure reached the last generation. The scripture itself tells us plainly its purpose. Its length speaks to more meaning than simply encouragement to these seven churches at that time in history alone. The fact that some of the symbols are similar to those described by Daniel, Ezekiel, and other OT prophets could mean that those prophets saw some of the same visions as John. While Revelation certainly was written and sent to the seven churches with encouragement for their day and ours, I couldn't get over the feeling (and I know that millions of others feel the same) that there is much more that God is telling us in His prophecy. So what is it that Revelation is telling us?

The easiest way for me to begin is to describe the conclusions that I have drawn from writing this book. These are the five keys to understanding Revelation. The first two Keys I have learned over my lifetime, the final three came to me during my devotional journey to understand Revelation. It is important to understand these Keys up front, because they are the underpinning for the discussion of Revelation that follows.

Key 1. God lives and loves us.

I mentioned earlier that the Holy Spirit touched me on my way home from high school. That was a defining moment in my life that I would like to share with you.

I was 15 years old and a member of my high school wrestling team. It was February, about 5:30 p.m., cold and dark. I was walking home about a half mile from the school on a lonely sidewalk. I could see my breath and my hair and ears were freezing having showered after practice. As I started to climb the hill before me, the cold and the fatigue from the practice started to get to me. Without even thinking I said a little prayer under my breath. "Dear Lord, it sure is cold." Then Spirit touched me. A wave of warmth spread across me from my toes to my head. I knew that God had answered my prayer. I started to run. I couldn't contain myself. I thanked God and ran the rest of the way home. I burst into the kitchen where my mother was cooking dinner and announced, " I am going to be a minister". That event is as clear to me today as it was then. And, while I did not initially become a minister, I am sure that God hears our prayers. He is concerned and involved in events here on earth. He lives and loves us.

But don't take my word for it. Revelation speaks about Jesus' direct involvement with people he cares about in his letters to the churches and elsewhere throughout the Bible. At the beginning of what Jesus tells the Churches in Revelation Chapter 2 verse 2 he says; "I know your deeds and your toil and perseverance,". Do you see it? Jesus is saying that he knows the deeds of this church at the time of John. In this and the following chapter, Jesus describes the issues with seven churches of John's day. He is telling John to write a letter to guide these churches years after he was crucified. These were real churches and John did write letters to them. The conclusion, Jesus was alive and loved us when John was on Patmos, when I was in high school, and will be forever. And, he loves you.

Key 2. The Bible is the word of God and he uses it to communicate with us.

As a Christian, I have been taught that the Bible is the word of God and that reading the Bible is key to learning about his laws and promises. But, what about all the Biblical commentators over the centuries who have interpreted the Bible to mean different things, dismissed it as allegorical, used archeological finds to support or change its meaning, debated its relevance to church doctrine, etc.? How could I know if all the right writings made it into the Bible, as we know it? How does God use the Bible to communicate with us? These questions plagued me for many years as I strived to get closer to God. The answer for me is that God uses the Bible to communicate with us in three ways; directly, through the words used, and through the Holy Spirit.

Is the Bible God's message? It has to be. What became clear to me is that in spite of all the questions that have been raised over the centuries, Bible scripture has been essentially the same since it was canonized about 1,600 years ago and word of mouth before that. Interpretations come and go, but the words in the Bible have remained essentially the same.

The Councils of Hippo and Cartage canonized the Bible as we know it in 397 AD / ACE. Sure, there have been insights from the Dead Sea Scrolls, etc, and certainly better more readable translations of the Bible have been written, but a person reading a portion of today's Bible 1600 years ago would recognize the text. So, if there is a living God that loves us and He wants us to have a book that He can use to communicate with us, then the Bible is the book as written. The proof that the existing Bible is God's message to us is that this is what has existed and He has used since Jesus came to the earth. No analysis can refute the fact that the Bible is what people have used to study and worship God since it was initially canonized. If God were going to send us a Christian instruction manual, He would want to make sure everyone had access to it over the centuries. The Bible, then, must contain the words that God wants us to read.

In addition, Jesus taught us that each word in the Bible is important and one word can tell us more than a simple reading of the scripture would yield. In Matthew 22 verse 32 Jesus used the word "am" in an Old Testament verse about the patriarchs to prove that the dead still live with God.

> "**I am** the God of Abraham, and the God of Isaac, and the God of Jacob'? He is not the God of the dead but of the living." And when the multitudes heard {this,} they were astonished at His teaching."

I too was astonished to learn that the tense of the word "am" is the way Jesus revealed one of the greatest mysteries of mankind in the OT. As Jesus pointed out, "am" is present tense and so are the lives of the Abraham, Isaac, and Jacob. To expand on this a bit further, the Greek word actually used in this verse is "eimi". Strong's Greek-Hebrew Dictionary, (copyright 1994), definition of this word is " The first person singular present indicative: A prolonged form of a primary and defective verb; I exist (used only when emphatic)". Jesus, in the New Testament, settled the debate on the resurrection of the dead by pointing out that "am" is present tense. Therefore, Abraham still lives and so does God.

Paul also shows in the book of Galatians that using a singular or plural word in the scripture is the key to understanding what God is telling us. In Galatians 3:16, Paul is discussing God's covenant with Abraham and says that the covenant is to Abraham and his seed not seeds, meaning one (Christ) not many (all of Abraham's descendants). Read Galatians for yourself.

These are just two examples of Jesus and Paul pointing out how a particular word used in scripture is important to discovering a deeper understanding of the scripture.

So, the words written in the Bible are a way in which God communicates with us both directly in the text and in a more subtle sense based on the words that God has inspired the authors to use.

I have used the same translation of the Bible throughout this book to retain a consistent translation and interpretation of the English from the Hebrew and Greek texts. I used the New American Standard Bible. Other translations will use slightly different words, but the underlying meanings will be the same.

The third way God uses the Bible to communicate with us is through the Holy Spirit. Over years of studying the Bible, I have found that I can read the same verses at different times and gain new and different understandings of what it is telling me. I know that the reason for some of this is because over time I learn more in other areas of the Bible that give me a greater, big picture, insight into things I read later. But this is not all that is going on. Somehow a scripture that I am reading triggers thoughts about what is going on in my life. The combination of the Biblical message and my life experience opens areas of thought that are beyond my thinking. I attribute this experience to the work of the Holy Spirit. God uses the Bible as a tool to engage real time with people who are open to his power and are searching for his insights. This is what I experienced as I wrote this book.

I conclude from this, that the Bible is the word of God and that He uses it to communicate with us on many levels including the choice of words used and the insights he gives to us directly. This is the second key to understanding Revelation.

Key 3. The Bible interprets itself.

The third assumption in this book is that the Bible often defines the symbols that it uses thereby interpreting itself. Revelation is full of amazing word pictures and symbols that seem difficult to interpret, but it also takes great pains to interpret itself. Some interpretations are immediate as in Revelation 4 verse 5: "And {there were} seven lamps of fire burning before the throne, which are the seven Spirits of God;" while other interpretations are found elsewhere in the Bible.

> Rev 12:9
> 9   And the great <u>dragon</u> was thrown down, the serpent of old who is called the <u>devil and Satan,</u> who deceives the whole world; he was thrown down to the earth, and his angels were thrown down with him.

> Rev 13:2
> 2   And the beast which I saw was like a leopard, and his feet were like {those} of a bear, and his mouth like the mouth of a lion. And the <u>dragon</u> gave him his power and his throne and great authority.

Here we see Revelation Chapter 12 Verse 9 defining who the dragon is and then we can understand in Chapter 13:2 Verse 2 who gave the beast his power.

For the purpose of this book, I have identified symbols in Revelation that the Bible defines for us and have used those definitions. In this way we can better understand what the Bible is telling us using its definitions not mine or someone else's. You can find a list of these interpretations in Appendix A.

<u>Key 4. Don't add or take away from the words in Revelation</u>.

To make sense of the book of Revelation, many authors of books on Revelation expand on the text or skip over sections that do not fit with traditional teachings. Revelation Chapter 22 is very specific about this:

> 18   I testify to everyone who hears the <u>words</u> of the prophecy of this book: if anyone adds to them, God shall add to him the plagues which are written in this book;

19   and if anyone takes away from the <u>words</u> of the book of this prophecy, God shall take away his part from the tree of life and from the holy city, which are written in this book.

Could this be clearer? Revelation is a prophecy not simply information to seven churches, and we should not add or delete any words from it. But how can we gain a deeper understand of Revelation without adding or deleting from it? I have highlighted the word "<u>words</u>" in the quote above because that is what led me to a deeper understanding of Revelation. Notice that it says words not verses or chapters or thoughts or concepts or events. This focus on words led me to the fundamental insight that is the foundation of this book, as I will describe in Key 5.

So, from this I conclude that I must use the entire text to understand Revelation. If part of the text doesn't fit then I don't have the answer. This led me to the 5th key, the greatest revelation in my devotional journey, and the reason that I began writing this book.

<u>Key 5. Revelation was written out of chronological order to seal it up until the end-times.</u>

As I pondered the book of Revelation, it seemed incomprehensible. Revelation appears to be a prophecy written to tell Christians throughout the centuries what will happen in advance of the end-times so that we will be prepared and keep the faith. It seems to be written chronologically from the time of John forward to the next world. Yet the stories of the harlot, various beasts, plagues, etc. do not tell a smooth flowing, understandable story. Many verses start with "Then" or contain "and then" that seems to indicate that the next events followed the preceding. But, the events described do not flow logically forward. Instead the story line seems to jump around. This contradiction between a book to tell Christians what will happen, yet presenting a book that is not clear, is a dilemma. Revelation is a true parable. People for thousands of years have read the words, but don't understand without God's interpretation.

One night while I lay in bed, my mind wrestled with how to understand these things. My spirit tingled as I read the admonition to not change the "words" as written in Revelation 22:19. Why focus on words? That got me thinking about what could be changed that would provide me greater insight if I could not change the words. As I read Jesus words about the end-times in the Gospels, the answer became clear. The words in Revelation are true, but the order of events presented there are not. It appears to be written in chronological order, but it is not. This is a way that God could give all mankind the same words to read over the ages, yet seal up Revelation's true meaning until the end-time. The key to understanding Revelation is to reorder it to correspond with the order of events described by Jesus in the Gospels, Matt 24:9-34, Mark 13: 9-31, and Luke 21:7-33. Jesus words in these Gospels tell us how to interpret Revelation. This sent tingles down my spine.

But, this led me to three questions. First, why would John write Revelation out of order? The answer to this question is that he didn't. He wrote it in the order of the visions that God showed him.

> Rev 1:10 – 11 "I was in the Spirit on the Lord's day, and I heard behind me a loud voice like {the sound} of a trumpet, saying, **'Write in a book what you see,** and send {it} to the seven churches"

But God did not show John the vision in the order in which the events described would take place, thereby sealing up the details of its meaning until the end-times. Revelation is, therefore, the chronological story that John saw as scenes in heaven, scenes on earth, flashbacks, and prophecies. The word "then" means what John saw next not necessarily what would happen next. John's experience is like watching a play where you see all the acts and scenes of the play, but not in order and then you are told to write what you saw. It is only by reordering these scenes that the true chronology of end-time events emerges. I believe that God did not want the true chronology to be known until the end-times, so that each generation would believe and look to the day of Christ's return even if it was actually to be hundreds of years in the future. As we enter the end-times, he wants us to know the straight story.

The second question is, if Revelation is out of order, how could we possibly know what order to put it in? As I began my efforts to discover how to reorder the text, I wanted to be sure that I was not reordering it to fit some preconceived idea as to what Revelation has to say. I worked under the assumption that if a scene didn't fit, that it was I who did not understand. For that reason, I began by using the original order unless there was a reason to change it and to use Jesus' words in the Gospels and the words in the text to signal what should be together. Here is an example of a time tag in the Gospels and in Revelation that shows how events can be synchronized:

> Mark 13:24-25 (NASB)
> 24 "But in those days, after **that** tribulation, THE **SUN** WILL BE DARKENED AND THE **MOON** WILL NOT GIVE ITS LIGHT,
> 25 AND THE **STARS WILL BE FALLING** from heaven, and the powers that are in the heavens will be shaken.

> Revelation 6:12-13 (NASB)
> 12 I looked when He broke the sixth seal, and there was a great earthquake; and the **sun** became black as sackcloth made of hair, and the whole **moon** became like blood;
> 13 and the **stars of the sky fell** to the earth, as a fig tree casts its unripe figs when shaken by a great wind.

Both Mark and Revelation are describing the same events. The reordered chapters came together in a way that was consistent with the Gospels. And, because the event of the stars falling has not happened in the past, this must be a prophecy for the future.

The third question was what did God mean when he said in Rev 1:1 that the events would happen shortly or in a short period of time? This has been a problem for scholars and readers alike since it was written. This has led scholars to believe that they must look at events in the first century to explain Revelation. This is also why every generation has believed that their generation will see the end of times. But these events did not happen in a short period of time from when Revelation was written. Is the revelation wrong, or is there another interpretation?

The text says that the revelation is to show His bondservants / followers / believers, but it does not say which ones. Most assume it means the churches to which John is writing. Another interpretation could be that it is addressed to the end-time bond-servants that see the things that Jesus is describing in Matt 24:9-34, Mark 13: 9-31, and Luke 21:7-33. The letters were sent to the seven churches to make sure that the prophecy was preserved. It became clear that Jesus is the key to understanding to whom the revelation is addressed. I believe that **God's** real audience is not the disciples Jesus is talking to in the Gospels, or the churches that John is writing to in Revelation, but the bondservants that see the signs that Jesus describes in the Gospels.

> Mark 13:29-30 (NASB)
> 29 "Even so, you too, when **you see these things happening,** recognize that He is near, right at the door.
> 30 "Truly I say to you, **this generation** will not pass away until all these things take place.

The literal reading of the revelation has helped all generations to get a glimpse of the end of the Biblical story and be assured that Christ will return in triumph, but the details of this parable have been sealed until the end-time generation.

Another revelation to me was that these three descriptions by Jesus to his disciples all say that "this generation" will see the end of it all. The word "this" is singular. This means that the bondservants he is speaking to "will see the end of it all" **within one generation.** The end-time generation will see all that Jesus describes in the Gospels and the events described in Revelation.

As I gained more and more insights from the Spirit, the scriptures began to open up and I received greater understanding. Each subsequent time through, the text and the Spirit opened more doors until the order and the meaning became clear. What emerged over many drafts is a chronology with distinct subdivisions that can be seen in the text based on God's involvement with his chosen people and recipients of His covenants, the Jews and the Christians. I also began to realize that Revelation not only tells the story of the end-times, but also why we are born, why good people suffer, the completion of God's covenant with the Jews as well as the Christians, and many more things.

To continue our metaphor of John seeing a play out of order, I will call these subdivisions Acts. The first Act includes all the events prior to the end-times. In Act 2, God and Satan are working through people on earth at the beginning of the end-times. In Act 3, God directly intervenes on earth while Christians are still on the earth. Act 4 begins God's direct intervention after Christians are removed from the earth. Acts 5 and 6 are events during the millennium and the new world respectively. Once these Acts were identified, it was relatively easy to order the Chapters of Revelation into these Acts and create a chronology of how events will unfold. When this was done, it became clear that there are three end-time tribulations described not one. The first is a tribulation of Christians by Satan, the beast. The second and third tribulations are by God on nonbelievers on earth. Using these concepts the reordered book of Revelation's Table of Contents reads like this.

Revelations Table of Contents
Reordered Revelations
Table of Contents

1.   Executive Summary - God
2.   Preface – John
3.   Happenings on earth and in Heaven prior to the end-times. This includes the tribulation that has happened to all people from the beginning of time, Tribulation 0.
4.   Happenings on earth and in Heaven at the beginning of the end-times but prior to God's direct intervention, End-Time Tribulation 1.
5.   Happenings on earth and in Heaven when God directly intervenes and Christians are still on the earth, End Time Tribulation 2.
6.   Happening on earth and in Heaven after Christians are removed from the earth, End-Time Tribulation 3.
7.   The millennium.
8.   The new world.

The result is a book of Revelation reordered into the following chapter order: 1, 2, 3, 12, 4, 5, 6a, 13, 17, 11a, 6b, 7, 8, 9a, 18, 9b, 14, 10, 11b, 15, 16, 19, 20, 21, 22.

The concept of this book can be illustrated as follows showing each of the Acts as a part of the pyramid starting from the past at the base leading to the future at the top.

Revelation Reordered

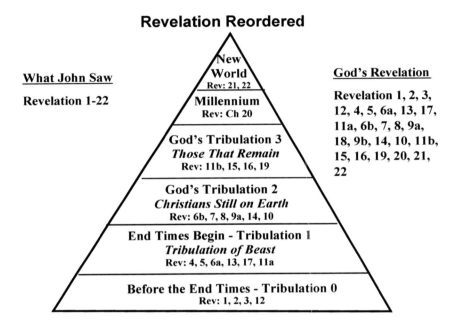

What John Saw

Revelation 1-22

New World
Rev: 21, 22

Millennium
Rev: Ch 20

God's Tribulation 3
Those That Remain
Rev: 11b, 15, 16, 19

God's Tribulation 2
Christians Still on Earth
Rev: 6b, 7, 8, 9a, 14, 10

End Times Begin - Tribulation 1
Tribulation of Beast
Rev: 4, 5, 6a, 13, 17, 11a

Before the End Times - Tribulation 0
Rev: 1, 2, 3, 12

God's Revelation

Revelation 1, 2, 3, 12, 4, 5, 6a, 13, 17, 11a, 6b, 7, 8, 9a, 18, 9b, 14, 10, 11b, 15, 16, 19, 20, 21, 22

Reading Revelation reordered in this way took me on a remarkable chronological journey through the end-times and provided me with many new insights. I will take you on this journey in the remainder of this book and use this graphic to remind you where we are in the story.

My hope is that your devotional search will be as rewarding as mine has been. And, that you will not be mislead as the end draws near.

Chapter 2. God's Executive Summary & John's Preamble

We begin our journey into Revelation by discussing each chapter of the reordered Revelation. In each chapter of this book, I will present a verse-by-verse discussion. My discussion and comments are in italics and the verses from Revelation are not. I have retained the original references so that you can see where the text comes from. In each succeeding chapter of the reordered Revelation, I explain why I have decided on this placement of the text to justify my reordering, I quote the reordered text, and propose some insights I have gained from the result. I also insert text from the Old and New Testament that is appropriate to the given section in Revelation thereby pulling together, in pertinent part, a Bible wide view of what is being said. I have underlined words in the biblical text that are pertinent to my discussion of insights, and used **bold** to highlight words that I want to highlight throughout the scripture. I do not add or delete any word from the Revelation text.

In Chapter 9, I present to you my case as to where we are in the Revelation chronology based on insights from the reordered Revelation and speculate on what lies ahead. I urge you not to skip to the end before you read the other chapters of this book. The insights that come from the discussions of the reordered Revelation are key to understanding where we might be in the chronology and what you need to understand to be prepared.

God's revelation is the important message not my speculation on what is happening today.

So lets begin.

Revelation's Executive Summary

Revelation Chapter 1 is the beginning of the book of Revelation and it also begins the reordered text. We begin our journey with God's Executive Summary, Verses 1-8. I call this God's Executive Summary because it contains the essentials of the book of Revelation and the Bible.

As I mentioned at the beginning of this book, I am a retired government executive. In government and at the top level of all major corporations, the executives don't have time to read everything they need to read to make important decisions. Imagine what all the President of the United Sates would have to read to make an informed decision on any subject. As a result, an executive summary is developed for each document that requires an executive decision. In my experience, it is usually best to keep this to one page or less. The trick is to get all the most important points of a document that may be hundreds of pages long into one page. I know an executive summary when I see one. God has put an executive summary of the Bible into the beginning of Revelation.

I will summarize to illustrate why I believe Verses 1-8 are God's Executive Summary then I will discuss this section in more detail. Verse 1 describes how the revelation comes to John, and Verse 2 tells us why. Verse 3 echoes the blessing in the final verses of revelation. Verse 4 says that the book is written by John to the churches. Verse 5 says that John received the revelation from God, the Spirit, and Christ and describes Christ's credentials. It also says that Christ loves us and saved us by his death. Verse 6 tells us the end of the revelation story and our future as

Christians; that we will be a kingdom and priests of God. Verse 7 tells the punch line of the revelation by describing how Christ will return and the fact that all those who ever lived will see him return including those who pierced him as he hung on the cross. Verse 8 is God's signature block and completes the executive summary to the Revelation. See for yourself.

Rev 1:1-20
CHAPTER 1

1   The Revelation of <u>Jesus Christ</u>, which <u>God gave Him</u> to show to His <u>bond-servants</u>, the things which must <u>shortly</u> take place; and He sent and communicated {it} by His angel to His <u>bond-servant</u> John,
2   who bore witness to the word of God and to the testimony of Jesus Christ, {even} to <u>all that he saw</u>.

If you read these verses closely they say that this is the revelation that God gave to Jesus Christ so that Christ could show his bond-servants what will happen. So this is actually God's revelation to Christ. And Christ sent it by his angel to John. God's plan was not only to inform Christ, but his bond-servants as well. Who are Bond Servants? Revelation 11:18 defines bond-servants as prophets, saints, and those who fear God's name. In this first verse of Revelation, God refers to John as a bond-servant of Christ because he bore witness to Jesus. He also was referring to you and me, John's brothers and sisters, if we fear God and bear witness to Christ.

In addition, God gave Jesus this revelation to show His followers / bond-servants "the things which must <u>shortly</u> take place…". This is why some scholars believe it is only addressing the original churches and why every generation has believed that their generation will see the end of times. But these events did not happen in a short period of time from when Revelation was written. The text says that the revelation is to show His bond-

servants, but it does not say which ones. As I said, most assume it means the churches. Another interpretation could be that it is addressed to the end-time bond-servants that see the things he is describing in Matt 24:9-34, Mark 13: 9-31, and Luke 21:7-33. In that case, it is only when we near the end-times that the revelation is to become fully known.

3   Blessed is he who reads and those who hear the <u>words</u> of the prophecy, and heed the things which are written in it; for the time is near.

Regardless of what the scholars say this verse says that Revelation is a prophecy. Revelation 22:18 tell us of the same blessing. So, Revelation begins and ends with the same message. Even if you can't read, you can receive this blessing if you act on what it tells us. Once again, don't take any <u>words</u> from the prophecy.

4   John to the seven churches that are in Asia: Grace to you and peace, from Him who is and who was and who is to come; and from the seven Spirits who are before His throne;

Revelation refers in various places to churches and synagogues. Churches refer to the church of Christ (Christians). While synagogues refer to the covenant with Abraham, the Jews. This verse, therefore, tells us that Revelation is written to Christians, but as you will see, it describes what will happen to fulfill God's covenant with the Jews as well.

Notice that "Him who is and who was and who is to come" is God the father not Jesus Christ. The seven Spirits are before the throne of God not Christ. The next verse, 5, says "and from Jesus Christ" not who is Jesus Christ.

5   and from Jesus Christ, the faithful witness, the first-born of the dead, and the ruler of the kings of the earth. To Him who loves us, and released us from our sins by His blood,

Verse 5 is the story of Jesus in two phrases. It is certainly an executive summary of who Jesus Christ is. How remarkable.

6   and He has made us {to be} a kingdom, priests to His God and Father; to Him {be} the glory and the dominion forever and ever. Amen.

How long has man wondered why we are here on earth? Here is the answer. Christ created us to be part of his kingdom and to be priests of God. This is the executive summary of who we are.

7   Behold, He is <u>coming with the clouds,</u> and every eye will see Him, <u>even those who pierced Him</u>; and all the tribes of the earth will mourn over Him. Even so. Amen.

This is a reference to Revelation 14:14 when Christ returns to earth. It also says that both the living and the dead, including those who crucified him, will see him when he returns to earth. The text ends with Amen to show that this is the end of what God has to say in his executive summary.

8   "I am the Alpha and the Omega," says the Lord God, "who is and who was and who is to come, the Almighty."

In this verse, God is telling us who he is. Interestingly, God told Moses that his name is "I Am".

```
Exod 3:13-15
13 Then Moses said to God, "Behold, I am
going to the sons of Israel, and I
shall say to them, 'The God of your fathers
has sent me to you.' Now they
```

```
may say to me, 'What is His name?' What
shall I say to them?"
14 And God said to Moses, "I AM WHO I AM";
and He said, "Thus you shall say to the sons
of Israel, 'I AM has sent me to you.'"
```

Can you see how verses across the Bible can bring insight to what you are reading in Revelation? Once we know that God's name is I AM, then we see that this is not only a statement from God, but also His signature block at the end of His Executive Summary. I would sign a document for my business:

Charles H. Huettner, President
Charles Huettner Associates, LLC

God signed His Executive summary and cover letter to the book of Revelation:

I AM, The Almighty
The Alpha and the Omega, who is and who was and who is to come.

I Am, (his name), The Almighty (His title), The Alpha and the Omega, who is and who was and who is to come (Who he is),

So, in these first 8 verses of Revelation we have the top level version of the book of Revelation and the Bible authored by God. This is the only portion of the Bible specifically dictated by God that includes his signature. Isn't it interesting that this executive summary would begin the final book in the canonized Bible. How appropriate that God would sign his inspired Bible.

If you only have time to read 8 verses of the Bible this is what you should read and thoroughly understand. What follows in this chapter is the Preface of the book written by John as directed by Jesus Christ.

Revelation's Preamble

9   I, John, your brother and <u>fellow partaker in the tribulation</u> and <u>kingdom</u> and **perseverance** {which are} in Jesus, was on the island called Patmos, because of the word of God and the testimony of Jesus.

Verses 1 – 8 were written by God. From verse 9 on, John is the author telling the story that he has been told to write. The remainder of Chapter 1 of Revelation is John setting the scene for his writing of what he has seen. This is where John has the opportunity to speak to us from his experience as a prophet, disciple, and friend of Jesus Christ on earth. It is his attempt to put Jesus Christ and his revelation into prospective.

Verse 9 may also be one of the most important verses in the Bible for people who have suffered a tragedy in their lives. It tells us what it is to be "in Christ". It is odd that most people, including myself, seem to skip over the first portion of this verse and focus on John being on Patmos. Yet the first portion of the verse is key to understanding Revelation and your life. With regard to Revelation, it is John's executive summary. If we reorder Verse 9 it plainly says that to be in Christ we will partake in tribulation. If we persevere then we will be part of his kingdom. This is the story of Revelation in a nut shell, and it is John's first sentence in the preamble to his book. The remainder of the book is filling in the details.

With regard to your life, I am sure that you have had things happen that have caused you to wonder why a loving God would allow this to happen; perhaps the death of a loved one, or a tragic disease, injury or injustice. What this verse is telling us is that to be "in Christ" you will go through tough times, adversities, tribulations, and it is up to you to persevere to enter His kingdom. This was the story of Jesus' life here on earth. Why should we expect something different for we who are Christ's followers?

*Those that turn away from Christ when times are tough fail to persevere and will fail to be part of Christ's kingdom. The gospel is full of verses that tell this story, such as the seed that falls on the rocky path (*Matthew 13:18-23*), yet here it is spoken plainly as part of the introduction to Revelation. The bottom line is that as far as God is concerned, the tribulation isn't the most important issue; it is how you respond to it that really counts.*

Verse 9 foreshadows what Christians will go through during the end-times. I believe the word "perseverance" is a key aspect to Revelation and to the Bible as a whole. Revelation 3:10 defines perseverance as keeping God's word through adversity to the point where God intervenes even unto death. Perseverance also implies action on our part. Look it up in the dictionary. It does not mean to throw up your hands and say "it is in God's hands". It means to keep working through the tough times and keep your faith that God is with you, because He is. This was a great insight to me. If you look at the number of times the word perseverance or a similar thought appears in the text, you see that it is a central theme for Christians in the end-times. I will highlight the word perseverance and similar words like overcome, keeping the faith, etc. throughout Revelation in **bold** *for you to see.*

So, if we are to be brothers of John in Christ, we will participate in the tribulation, be part of Christ's kingdom, and be asked to persevere. To say it another way, horrible events are coming as part of end-time tribulations the likes of which have never been seen before. They are coming to establish Christ's kingdom. To be saved, believers must persevere in order to take part in the kingdom and be priests of God. The fire of tribulation refines us all. Christ was the first to go through this, and we must also go through it as well to be like him.

10   I was in the Spirit on the Lord's Day, and I heard behind me a loud voice like {the sound} of a trumpet,
11   saying, "Write in a book what you see, and send {it} to the seven churches: to Ephesus and to Smyrna and to Pergamum and to Thyatira and to Sardis and to Philadelphia and to Laodicea."

Here John begins his preface by telling us where he is and what he has been told to do. Notice here that John is directed to write the book of Revelations as he sees it (as it is shown to him). Not necessarily as it will occur during the end-times.

12   And I turned to see the voice that was speaking with me. And having turned I saw seven golden lampstands;
13   and in the middle of the lampstands one like a son of man, clothed in a robe reaching to the feet, and girded across His breast with a golden girdle.
14   And His head and His hair were **white** like white wool, like snow; and His eyes were like a flame of fire;
15   and His feet {were} like burnished bronze, when it has been caused to glow in a furnace, and His voice {was} like the sound of many waters.
16   And in His right hand He held seven stars; and out of His mouth came a sharp two-edged sword; and His face was like the sun shining in its strength.

Any good preamble gives the background first. This is it. It begins in the present day when John was praying. It describes the seven churches and then it describes a vision of lampstands that Revelation 1:20 define as Churches. I don't think it is coincidental that churches are symbolized by lampstands whose purpose is to enlighten. Lampstands also play a significant role in Jewish faith and are a perfect symbol of the transition from the old covenant with Israel to the new covenant through Jesus Christ.

So, John is to write to the churches and he is seeing a vision of the son of man standing in their midst. The description of the son of man in this vision is remarkably close to the description Daniel uses in his vision of the end-times. I will <u>underline</u> the similarities of imagery. There are also similarities in message and theme. The preamble to Daniel's vision is a parallel to the preamble of John's. This is a way to confirm that Chapters 10-12 of Daniel's prophecy relates to the same events described in Revelation. This connection helps us to better understand both scriptures. This will be important later because the New Testament specifically refers to Daniel's prophecy regarding the end-times.

Dan 10:1-8
CHAPTER 10

1   In the third year of Cyrus king of Persia a message was revealed to Daniel, who was named Belteshazzar; and the message was true and {one of} great conflict, but he understood the message and had an understanding of the vision.
2   In those days I, Daniel, had been mourning for three entire weeks.
3   I did not eat any tasty food, nor did meat or wine enter my mouth, nor did I use any ointment at all, until the entire three weeks were completed.
4   And on the twenty-fourth day of the first month, while I was by the bank of the great river, that is, the Tigris,
5   I lifted my eyes and looked, and behold, there was a certain man <u>dressed in linen</u>, whose waist was <u>girded with {a belt of} pure gold</u> of Uphaz.
6   His body also was like beryl, his face had the appearance of lightning, his <u>eyes were like flaming torches</u>, his arms and <u>feet like the gleam of polished bronze</u>, and

the sound of his <u>words like the sound of a tumult</u>.

7   Now I, Daniel, alone saw the vision, while the men who were with me did not see the vision; nevertheless, a great dread fell on them, and they ran away to hide themselves.

8   So I was left alone and saw this great vision; yet no strength was left in me, for my natural color turned to a deathly pallor, and I retained no strength.

9   But I heard the sound of his words; and as soon as I heard the sound of his words, <u>I fell into a deep sleep on my face, with my face to the ground.</u>

10   <u>Then behold, a hand touched me</u> and set me trembling on my hands and knees.

11   And he said to me, "O Daniel, man of high esteem, understand the words that I am about to tell you and stand upright, for I have now been sent to you." And when he had spoken this word to me, I stood up trembling.

17   And when I saw Him, <u>I fell at His feet as a dead man. And He laid His right hand upon me, saying, "Do not be afraid</u>; I am the first and the last,

18   and the living One; and I was dead, and behold, I am alive forevermore, and I have the keys of death and of Hades.

We know that this is Christ, "living One; and I was dead" speaking to John, quoting God, because he says I am the first and last which we know to be God from verse 8 above. And in fact that is exactly what Revelation Chapter 1 Verse 1 says it is, God's revelation to Christ who gives it to John.

19   "Write therefore the <u>things which you have seen,</u> and the <u>things which **are**,</u> and the <u>things which shall take place **after** these things.</u>

*Verse 19 provides us with the broad layout of Revelation and a clue to how it should be reordered. It says that John is first directed to write what he sees, scene-by-scene as he is shown. Then he is told what he will see; things that are and things that will take place after these things, i.e. things prior to the end-times and events of the end-times. So there are two major time periods that he will write about. The first includes things that are happening in the normal course of life from John's day up to the end-times (things that **are**) and then he will describe the things that will happen during the end-times and beyond (take place **after** these things). These are clues as to how to reorder Revelation that I will continue to describe as we proceed.*

20   "As for the mystery of the seven stars which you saw in My right hand, and the seven golden lampstands: the seven stars are the angels of the seven churches, and <u>the seven lampstands are the seven churches</u>.

John ends his preamble saying that each church is symbolized by a lampstand. Throughout the Bible, God is symbolized by light. Therefore, the churches hold the light.

Verse 20 is an example of how the Bible defines itself. This ends John's preface to the book of Revelation and leads us to the beginning of the Revelation; what will take place before the end-times from God's point of view.

Revelation Reordered

New
World
Rev: 21, 22
Millennium
Rev: Ch 20
God's Tribulation 3
Those That Remain
Rev: 11b, 15, 16, 19
God's Tribulation 2
Christians Still on Earth
Rev: 6b, 7, 8, 9a, 14, 10
End Times Begin - Tribulation 1
Tribulation of Beast
Rev: 4, 5, 6a, 13, 17, 11a
Before the End Times - Tribulation 0
Rev: 1, 2, 3, 12

Chapter 3. Act 1 - Prior to the End-Times

We now begin the first Act of God's revelation. Revelation Chapters 2, 3, and 12 comprise the first group of Revelation Chapters in the reordered Revelation as I shall describe. Act 1, Scene 1, begins with John's letters to the churches. It is in the same order as the book of Revelation as John saw the visions.

Tribulation 0

Chapter 2 and 3 of Revelation are clearly set in the times before the end-times; the times that "are". This is shown by the description of what Christ is seeing as he reviews the record of each church and his guidance to the church to ready itself for the future. This is the beginning of the Revelation story.

Chapters 2 and 3 begin with how things are in John's time. For this reason, they appear in the reordered Revelation after the Executive Summary and Preface of the book. As I searched through the remainder of Revelation, I discovered that Chapter 12 also describes what happened before the end-times so it too is included in this Act as scene 3. Therefore, Chapters 2, 3, and 12 comprise the first group of Revelation Chapters in the reordered Revelation. This is because they describe events that are happening before the end-times begin. This concept of grouping Revelation chapters based on the time they represent is a concept that will help us to group other sections of

Revelation after these in order to tell the Revelation story in the order in which events will occur.

Notice that each church has a tribulation to face. I have labeled this Tribulation 0 because it comes before the end-times. Tribulation 0 represents all the heartaches, horrors, and challenges that churches and people have faced from the beginning of time up to the end-times. I make this point because Christ's focus on perseverance in speaking to each church is something that has been key to being like Christ from the beginning, not simply during the end-times.

Rev 2:1-29
CHAPTER 2

1   "To the angel of the church in <u>Ephesus</u> write: the One who holds the seven stars in His right hand, the One who walks among the seven golden lampstands, says this:
2   'I know your deeds and your toil and **perseverance,** and that you cannot endure evil men, and you put to the test those who call themselves apostles, and they are not, and you found them {to be} false;
3   and you have **perseverance** and have endured for My name's sake, and have not grown weary.
4   'But I have {this} against you, that you have left your first love.
5   'Remember therefore from where you have fallen, and repent and do the deeds you did at first; or else I am coming to you, and will remove your lampstand out of its place-- unless you repent.
6   'Yet this you do have, that you hate the deeds of the Nicolaitans, which I also hate.
7   'He who has an ear, let him hear what the Spirit says to the churches. To him who **overcomes,** I will grant to eat of the tree of life, which is in the Paradise of God.'

*Christ's statement to the first church mentions apostles. This has led some who have studied Revelation to conclude that each church in the list is a phase that the church in general will go through over time with Ephesus representing the early Christian church and Laodicea, the last church mentioned, being the church of today. I believe that it is what it says it is. These are churches that existed then, as well as being examples of churches that exist today. Clearly Christ and John would only write to a church to describe a problem or accomplishment that existed. There are churches today that have clergy who call themselves apostles and they are not. Notice that **overcome** is another word for **persevere,** so I show it in **bold** as well.*

8   "And to the angel of the church in **Smyrna** write: The first and the last, who was dead, and has come to life, says this:
9   'I know your tribulation and your poverty (but you are rich), and the blasphemy by those who say they are Jews and are not, but are a synagogue of Satan.

Here is where Revelation defines the use of the word synagogue in Revelation. Synagogue is used to refer to the Jews who follow the Jewish faith and laws, where churches can be defined as believers in Christ (called by Christ's name; Christians). Jews that come to believe in Christ become Christians and some of their Synagogues become Churches. So these verses are telling us that the Smyrna Church was being persecuted by the Jewish Synagogues that did not believe in Christ. Revelation is the final chapter for Christians and Jews.

10   'Do not fear what you are about to suffer. Behold, the devil is about to cast some of you into prison, that you may be tested, and you will have tribulation ten days. Be **faithful** <u>until death,</u> and I will give you the crown of life.
11   'He who has an ear, let him hear what the Spirit says to the churches. He who **overcomes** <u>shall not be hurt by the second death.</u>'

Note that verse 11 says that he who overcomes will not be <u>hurt</u> by the second death. This implies that believers who die prior to the end-time will face the second death, but will not be hurt by it. As we will see later, God's people who die during the end-times will not face the second death. Their perseverance will lead to life with Christ during the Millennium. This verse also shows that God may allow tribulation for believers that include death.

Can you see in your mind Christ speaking to each church with its angel receiving these instructions? This is Christ speaking not only to the churches of John's day, but also to all the churches that will rise up until the end-time.

12   "And to the angel of the church in <u>Pergamum</u> write: The One who has the sharp two-edged sword says this:
13   'I know where you dwell, where Satan's throne is; and you hold fast My name, and did not deny My faith, even in the days of Antipas, My witness, My faithful one, who was killed among you, where Satan dwells.
14   'But I have a few things against you, because you have there some who hold the teaching of Balaam, who kept teaching Balak to put a stumbling block before the sons of Israel, to eat things sacrificed to idols, and to commit {acts of} immorality.
15   'Thus you also have some who in the same way hold the teaching of the Nicolaitans.
16   'Repent therefore; or else I am coming to you quickly, and I will make war against them with the sword of My mouth.
17   'He who has an ear, let him hear what the Spirit says to the churches. To him who **overcomes**, to him I will give {some} of the hidden manna, and I will give him a **white** stone, and a new name written on the stone which no one knows but he who receives it.'

*Notice here that the gift is a stone that is white. You will see that the term white is significant throughout Revelation. **White*** *represents pure, free from sin, God's. For this reason I will highlight it in bold as well.*

18   "And to the angel of the church in <u>Thyatira</u> write: The Son of God, who has eyes like a flame of fire, and His feet are like burnished bronze, says this:
19   'I know your deeds, and your love and faith and service and **perseverance,** and that your deeds of late are greater than at first.
20   'But I have {this} against you, that you tolerate the woman Jezebel, who calls herself a prophetess, and she teaches and leads My <u>bond-servants</u> astray, so that they commit {acts of} immorality and eat things sacrificed to idols.
21   'And I gave her time to repent; and she does not want to repent of her immorality.
22   'Behold, I will cast her upon a bed {of sickness} and those who commit adultery with her into great tribulation, unless they repent of her deeds.
23   'And I will kill her children with pestilence; and all the churches will know that I am He who searches the minds and hearts; and I will give to each one of you according to your deeds.
24   'But I say to you, the rest who are in Thyatira, who do not hold this teaching, who have not known the deep things of Satan, as they call them-- I place no other burden on you.
25   'Nevertheless what you have, **hold fast** until I come.
26   'And he who **overcomes**, and he who keeps My deeds until the end, to him I will give authority over the nations;

That is to say, give him authority in Christ's kingdom. These verses foretell what is in store for us if we persevere and become part of Christ's kingdom. They tell us that life in the next world will be a life of active involvement ruling nations and perhaps worlds as Christ rules the earth. We will be part of Christ's government for the universe. This is a Christian's ultimate role. Read on.

27   and he shall rule them with a rod of iron, as the vessels of the potter are broken to pieces, as I also have received {authority} from My Father;
28   and I will give him the morning star.
29   'He who has an ear, let him hear what the Spirit says to the churches.'

Rev 3:1-22
CHAPTER 3

1   "And to the angel of the church in <u>Sardis</u> write: He who has the seven Spirits of God, and the seven stars, says this: 'I know your deeds, that you have a name that you are alive, but you are dead.
2   'Wake up, and strengthen the things that remain, which were about to die; for I have not found your deeds completed in the sight of My God.
3   'Remember therefore what you have received and heard; and keep {it,} and repent. If therefore you will not wake up, I will come like a thief, and you will not know at what hour I will come upon you.
4   'But you have a few people in Sardis who have not soiled their garments; and they will walk with Me in **white**; for they are worthy.
5   'He who **overcomes** shall thus be clothed in **white** garments; and I will not erase his name from the book of life, and I will confess his name before My Father, and before His angels.
6   'He who has an ear, let him hear what the Spirit says to the churches.'
7   "And to the angel of the church in <u>Philadelphia</u> write: He who is holy, who is true, who has the key of David, who opens and no one will shut, and who shuts and no one opens, says this:
8   'I know your deeds. Behold, I have put before you an open door which no one can shut, because you have a little power, and have kept My word, and have not denied My name.

9   'Behold, I will cause {those} of the synagogue of Satan, who say that they are Jews, and are not, but lie-- behold, I will make them to come and bow down at your feet, and to know that I have loved you.

> Matt 25:15-24
> 20   "And the one who had received the five talents came up and brought five more talents, saying, 'Master, you entrusted five talents to me; see, I have gained five more talents.'
> 21   "His master said to him, 'Well done, good and faithful slave; you were faithful with a few things, I will put you in charge of many things, enter into the joy of your master.'

10   'Because you have kept the word of My **perseverance**, I also will keep you from the hour of testing, that {hour} which is about to come upon the whole world, to test those who dwell upon the earth.

Note here that Christ is telling the faithful people of Philadelphia that he will keep them from the hour when the whole world is tested because they have persevered. God will test the whole world during Tribulation 2, as you will see later.

11   'I am coming quickly; **hold fast** what you have, in order that no one take your crown.
12   'He who **overcomes**, I will make him a pillar in the temple of My God, and he will not go out from it anymore; and I will write upon him the name of My God, and the name of the city of My God, the new Jerusalem, which comes down out of heaven from My God, and My new name.
13   'He who has an ear, let him hear what the Spirit says to the churches.'
14   "And to the angel of the church in Laodicea write: The Amen, the faithful and true Witness, the Beginning of the creation of God, says this:

15   'I know your deeds, that you are neither cold nor hot; I would that you were cold or hot.

16   'So because you are lukewarm, and neither hot nor cold, I will spit you out of My mouth.

Lip service doesn't work with Christ. Each of us will face tribulation and we must persevere or lose out on being part of Christ's kingdom.

17   'Because you say, "I am rich, and have become wealthy, and have need of nothing," and you do not know that you are wretched and miserable and poor and blind and naked,

18   I advise you to buy from Me gold refined by fire, that you may become rich, and **white** garments, that you may clothe yourself, and {that} the shame of your nakedness may not be revealed; and eye salve to anoint your eyes, that you may see.

19   <u>'Those whom I love, I reprove and discipline</u>; be zealous therefore, and repent.

20   'Behold, I stand at the door and knock; if anyone hears My voice and opens the door, I will come in to him, and will dine with him, and he with Me.

21   'He who **overcomes** *(perseveres),* I will grant to him to sit down with Me on My throne, **as I also overcame** and sat down with My Father on His throne.

22   <u>'He who has an ear, let him hear what the Spirit says to the churches.</u>' "

I will make a final comment about John's letters to the churches. What is it that he who has an ear should hear? It is the key word that appears in each letter. Each letter contains the admonition to persevere.

Introducing the Forces of Evil

Revelation starts in Chapters 1,2, and 3 by introducing and defining God, Christ, John, angels, churches, etc. Now it is time

to introduce Israel and the force of evil. Chapter 12 comes naturally after Chapter 3 because it is clearly set at a time before the end-times, times as they "are". Chapters 2 and 3 describe the churches, this chapter introduces Satan. Chapter 12 provides the background of Satan's conflict with God, Christ, Israel, and us leading up to the end-times.

Rev 12:1-17
CHAPTER 12

1   And a great sign appeared in heaven: a <u>woman</u> clothed with the sun, and the moon under her feet, and on her head a <u>crown of twelve stars</u>;
2   and she was <u>with child</u>; and she cried out, being in labor and in pain to give birth.
3   And another sign appeared in heaven: and behold, a great **red** <u>dragon</u> having <u>seven heads and ten horns</u>, and on his heads {were} seven diadems.
4   And his tail swept away a <u>third of the stars</u> of heaven, and threw them to the earth. And the <u>dragon</u> stood before the <u>woman</u> who was about to give birth, so that when she gave birth he might devour her child.
5   And she gave birth to a son, a male {child} who is to rule all the nations with a rod of iron; and her child was caught up to God and <u>to His throne</u>.

Could the woman be anything other than Israel? Revelation 1:20 defines stars as angels that were associated with the churches, here the twelve stars in the crown represent angels associated with the twelve tribes of Israel. Israel is the woman who gave birth to Jesus Christ who is caught up to God's throne as you can see in Verse 5. It is plainly shown here that these verses are speaking to a time when Christ was born, prior to the end-times. This proves that this section of Revelation should be placed with Chapters 2 and 3 prior to the end-times.

If the woman is Israel and the child is Christ who is the dragon? Read on. Verse 9 tells you plainly that it is Satan and the stars that were swept away are his angels. Reading verse 4 and 9 together show that one third of the angels in heaven went with Satan to earth! That's a lot of evil in this world, and this occurs prior to the end-times.

6   And the <u>woman</u> fled into the wilderness where she had a place prepared by God, so that there she might be nourished for one thousand two hundred and sixty days.

I believe that this is describing the diffusion of the Jews around the world after the Roman Empire conquered Israel and later disintegrated. History shows that the Jews have been persecuted, but survived perhaps because they were not a nation from Roman times until Israel was reformed in 1948. Read on. I will show you more about this.

7   And there was war in heaven, Michael and his angels waging war with the <u>dragon</u>. And the <u>dragon</u> and his angels waged war,
8   and they were not strong enough, and there was no longer a place found for them in heaven.
9   And the great <u>dragon</u> was thrown down, the serpent of old who is <u>called the devil and Satan, who deceives the whole world</u>; he was thrown down to the earth, and his angels were thrown down with him.

So the timeline is that Christ is born, Israel is diffused into the nations yet preserved by God, Michael defeats Satan and throws him and 1/3 of the angels to earth, and Satan makes war with both Jews and Christians as you will see. Notice that God is saying here that Satan deceives the whole world. That includes you and me. This is why understanding Revelation is so important.

10   And I heard a loud voice in heaven, saying, "Now the salvation, and the power, and the kingdom of our God and the authority of His Christ have come, for the accuser of our brethren has been thrown down, who accuses them before our God day and night.

11   "And they **overcame** him because of the blood of the Lamb and because of the word of their testimony, and they did not love their life even to death.

12   "For this reason, rejoice, O heavens and you who dwell in them. Woe to the earth and the sea, because the devil has come down to you, having great wrath, knowing that he has {only} a short time."

13   And when the <u>dragon</u> saw that he was thrown down to the earth, he persecuted the <u>woman who gave birth to the male {child.}</u>

14   And the two wings of the great eagle were given to the woman, in order that she might fly into the wilderness to her place, where she was nourished for a time and times and half a time, from the presence of the serpent.

15   And the serpent poured water like a river out of his mouth after the woman, so that he might cause her to be swept away with the flood.

16   And the earth helped the woman, and the earth opened its mouth and drank up the river which the <u>dragon</u> poured out of his mouth.

I puzzled over verses 6, 15 and 16 trying to relate what is said in them to history. If this is part of the Act prior to the end-times portion of Revelation, then there must be some way to determine that this already happened. Then I discovered Revelation 17:15 which defined waters as people. The flood described here is not water. It was a flood of people that would overwhelm and in other ways sweep Israel away. This is similar to what Daniel talks about in Chapter 11 Verse 40. But, in 1948, after WWII and the death of many people, the nations reestablished Israel in spite of Satan's efforts to "sweep it away". Could the two wings of the eagle mentioned in Verse 14 be Great Britain who founded Israel and the USA who has maintained and protected her since she was formed?

17   And the <u>dragon</u> was enraged with the woman, and went off to make war with the rest of her offspring, who keep the commandments of God and hold to the testimony of Jesus.

So the dragon has been against the Jews since Christ was born. Now, since Israel is reestablished and it is clear that he could not sweep Israel away, we see in verse 17 that Satan turns his attention to Christians; those who hold to the testimony of Jesus. The end-times are Satan's last ditch effort to eradicate both Jews and Christians.

Revelation Chapter 12 is the big picture history of the world from God's perspective. Clearly Chapter 12 describes events prior to the end-times. It shows the conflict between God and Satan since the birth of Christ. Now the stage is set to move to the end- times.

Revelation Reordered

New
World
Rev: 21, 22
Millennium
Rev: Ch 20
God's Tribulation 3
Those That Remain
Rev: 11b, 15, 16, 19
God's Tribulation 2
Christians Still on Earth
Rev: 6b, 7, 8, 9a, 14, 10
End Times Begin - Tribulation 1
Tribulation of Beast
Rev: 4, 5, 6a, 13, 17, 11a
Before the End Times - Tribulation 0
Rev: 1, 2, 3, 12

Chapter 4. Act 2 - Beginning of the End-Times

Up to this point, Revelation has introduced most of the principles in the Revelation story and described a history of the church, Satan's involvement with the Christians and Jews, and the secular world up to the end-times. Revelation now begins to address what will happen "after these things".

The End-Times Action Starts in Heaven

Rev 4:1-11
CHAPTER 4

1	After these things I looked, and behold, a door {standing} open in heaven, and the first voice which I had heard, like {the sound} of a trumpet speaking with me, said, "Come up here, and I will show you what must take place after these things."

Note that John specifically begins this chapter using the same wording that Christ used in telling him what to do in Rev 1:19. "These things" are the things that precede the end times that we have just discussed.

2	Immediately I was in the Spirit; and behold, a throne was standing in heaven, and One sitting on the throne.

3   And He who was sitting {was} like a jasper stone and a sardius in appearance; and {there was} a rainbow around the throne, like an emerald in appearance.

This is God's description of himself....his self portrait. So what does jasper stone and sardius look like?

Jasper is an opaque and fine grained variety of Chalcedony. It is found in all colors including: red, brown, pink, yellow, green, grey/white and shades of blue and purple. It often contains organic material and mineral oxides, which give it interesting patterns, bands and colors. Many of these patterns resemble landscapes with mountains and valleys, thus the name "picture" is part of the name of many well know jaspers. Perhaps like the landscape of Earth. The modern day term for sardius is red ruby.

4   And around the throne {were} twenty-four thrones; and upon the thrones {I saw} <u>twenty-four elders</u> sitting, clothed in **white** garments, and golden crowns on their heads.

Who are these twenty-four elders? I believe that they are the twelve Jewish patriarchs and the twelve apostles. I further believe that the twelve tribes of Israel represent the first covenant that God made with Israel and the twelve apostles represent the new covenant through Jesus Christ. I believe this because In Matthew, Jesus told his disciples that they too would be on thrones judging Israel.

> Matt 19:28
> 28   And Jesus said to them, "Truly I say to you, that you who have followed Me, in the regeneration when the Son of Man will sit on His glorious throne, you **also** shall sit upon twelve thrones, judging the twelve tribes of Israel.

Most people would read the word "also" in this verse to mean that the apostles would sit with Jesus (the Son of Man). It could also mean that they will join Jesus and the twelve patriarchs. Here is another example of gaining a larger view of what God is telling us by bringing together Biblical verses that address the same subject matter.

5   And from the throne proceed flashes of lightning and sounds and peals of thunder. And {there were} seven <u>lamps</u> of fire burning before the throne, <u>which are the seven Spirits of God;</u>

Revelation 1:20 defines lamp stands as Churches. This verse defines lamps as Spirits of God. So it seems clear that the Churches are meant to hold the Spirit to enlighten its members.

6   and before the throne {there was,} as it were, a sea of glass like crystal; and in the center and around the throne, four living creatures full of eyes in front and behind.

As we described before, water/sea in Revelation symbolizes people. The sea of glass is all of God's chosen people who have ever died. I believe that your loved ones who have died are before the throne of God today. And because it is a sea of glass, they can see God and what is happening before his throne. I will describe why I believe this in greater detail later.

7   And the first creature {was} like a lion, and the second creature like a calf, and the third creature had a face like that of a man, and the fourth creature {was} like a flying eagle.
8   And the four living creatures, each one of them having six wings, are full of eyes around and within; and day and night they do not cease to say, "Holy, holy, holy, {is} the Lord God, the Almighty, who was and who is and who is to come."

9   And when the living creatures give glory and honor and thanks to Him who sits on the throne, to Him who lives forever and ever,

10   the twenty-four elders will fall down before Him who sits on the throne, and will worship Him who lives forever and ever, and will cast their crowns before the throne, saying,

11   "Worthy art Thou, our Lord and our God, to receive glory and honor and power; for Thou didst create all things, and because of Thy will they existed, and were created."

The Book of Life Revealed

Rev 5:1-14
CHAPTER 5

1   And I saw in the right hand of Him who sat on the throne a book written inside and on the back, sealed up with seven seals.

2   And I saw a strong angel proclaiming with a loud voice, "Who is worthy to open the book and to break its seals?"

3   And no one in heaven, or on the earth, or under the earth, was able to open the book, or to look into it.

4   And I {began} to weep greatly, because no one was found worthy to open the book, or to look into it;

5   and one of the elders said to me, "Stop weeping; behold, the Lion that is from the tribe of Judah, the Root of David, has overcome so as to open the book and its seven seals."

6   And I saw between the throne (with the four living creatures) and the elders a Lamb standing, as if slain, having seven horns and <u>seven eyes, which are the seven Spirits of God</u>, sent out into all the earth.

The Root of David and the Lamb are Christ. Here the Spirits of God are symbolized as eyes that God has sent out to all the earth. In the last chapter the Spirits were lamps. This is God's way to telling us that the Spirits both enlighten the people of his church and oversee all that happens on earth. The Holy Spirit is the connection between God and individuals. Notice too that the Lamb is Christ and it is He that sends out the Spirit just as we are told he did in the Gospels and in Acts.

7   And He came, and He took {it} out of the right hand of Him who sat on the throne.

This makes it clear that it is God sitting on the throne and Christ before the throne.

8   And when He had taken the book, the four living creatures and the twenty-four elders fell down before the Lamb, having each one a harp, and golden bowls full of <u>incense, which are the prayers of the saints</u>.
9   And they sang a new song, saying, "Worthy art Thou to take the book, and to break its seals; for Thou wast slain, and didst purchase for God with Thy blood {men} from every tribe and tongue and people and nation.
10   "And Thou hast <u>made **them** {to be} a kingdom and priests to our God</u>; and they will reign upon the earth."

This is a place where my spiritual journey gave me a great Ah HA. I had read these first 10 verses of Chapter 5 hundreds of times and thought it was telling me that Jesus (the Lamb) received this book and was worthy because he persevered unto death. As a result, he purchased / saved people from all nations, races and cultures. This all seemed straightforward to me until I began writing this book and paid closer attention to the words used. There is a deeper meaning. While working on a draft of this book, I stumbled over the word "them" in verse 10. But who are the "them" that verse 10 refers to? Them must refer to those purchased for God by Christ. Then why would this vision of the heavenly host rejoicing over Christ purchasing people for God be in the scripture that is focused on Christ breaking seals on a book?

I believe that the book with the seven seals is the "Book-of-Life". Verse 9 speaks to those purchased for God. Reread Chapter 5 verses 1-10 again with this thought in mind. It essentially says that no one can open the book or look into it except Jesus Christ. It then says that he can see inside because he died for us. So only those who Christ died for can be in the book. It then says, "thou hast made them (the people whose names are in the book) to be a kingdom and priests to God. This is the believers destiny as described in Revelation 1:5. Christ has the book of life in his hand and he is the only one found worthy to open it because he is the person who took the sins of all the people who are in the book to the cross with him. He knows them all.

If this book is the book of life, then what are the seals? The seals are the final acts that need to be completed before the book can be opened. They are the final end-time events that will result in the book of life open and ready to reward the saints. The events that result from breaking each seal are what Revelation Chapters 6-19 are about.

11   And I looked, and I heard the voice of many angels around the throne and the living creatures and the elders; and the number of them was myriads of myriads, and thousands of thousands,

Think about the fact that Satan has 1/3 of this many angels here on earth (Rev 12:4).

12   saying with a loud voice, "Worthy is the Lamb that was slain to receive power and riches and wisdom and might and honor and glory and blessing."
13   And every created thing which is in heaven and on the earth and under the earth and on the sea, and all things in them, I heard saying, "To Him who sits on the throne, and to the Lamb, {be} blessing and honor and glory and dominion forever and ever."

14   And the four living creatures kept saying, "Amen." And the elders fell down and worshiped.

> 1 Cor 15:20-28
> 20   But now Christ has been raised from the dead, the first fruits of those who are asleep.
> 21   For since by a man {came} death, by a man also {came} the resurrection of the dead.
> 22   For as in Adam all die, so also in Christ all shall be made alive.
> 23   But each in his own order: Christ the first fruits, after that those who are Christ's at His coming, *(persevere through the end-times)*
> 24   then {comes} the end, when He delivers up the kingdom *(All of those whose names are written in the seven sealed book of life.)*
> to the God and Father, when He has abolished all rule and all authority and power
> 25   For He must reign until He has put all His enemies under His feet.
> 26   The last enemy that will be abolished is death.
> 27   For He has put all things in subjection under His feet. But when He says, "All things are put in subjection," it is evident that He is excepted who put all things in subjection to Him.
> 28   And when all things are subjected to Him, then the Son Himself also will be subjected to the One who subjected all things to Him, that God may be all in all.

These verses of Corinthians explain why Christ needs to break the seals in heaven. The end-time actions that result from the seals being broken are what will take place to abolish all rule, authority, and power here on earth. As we shall see later, at the seventh trumpet Christ returns to earth to abolish God's enemies, and the last is death and Hades. In the end, Christ will be all powerful because God made it possible, and then Christ will offer it all back to God. Could there be a better description of Love?

End -Time Events Begin on Earth

Rev 6:1-11
CHAPTER 6

1 And I saw when the Lamb broke one of the seven seals, and I heard one of the four living creatures saying as with a voice of thunder, "Come."
2 And I looked, and behold, a **white horse**, and he who sat on it had a bow; and a crown was given to him; and he went out conquering, and to conquer.

If the scroll is the Book of Life, then the seals are what will happen before Christ opens the book. Opening the first seal is the first action in Heaven that Revelations says has an effect on earth and it should be the first sign to us that the end-times have begun. Let's explore this first seal in some detail.

First we are talking about a white horse. White is the color of purity and good in Revelations. There are too many verses that relate the word white as good for me to list here. Some I have highlighted in bold previously. See for yourself as you read on through the text. Every time white is used it is a sign of good, or Godly. Christ's head and hair are white in Chapter 1 Verse 14. The 24 elders described in Chapter 4 Verse 4 are clothed in white garments. People who are saved will put on white robes, etc. So where many interpreters of Revelation view the breaking of this first seal as something bad, I believe that the person riding the white horse is doing God's work. The white horse is beginning God's end-time plan.

The second point is that the rider is carrying a bow. This is the only place in the New Testament that a bow is mentioned. Why a bow when in most every other case a sword is the weapon used to make the point? I believe that a bow is used because the person riding the white horse will strike from a distance as opposed to up close and personal when a sword is used. A bow, perhaps, represents a weapon such as an aircraft or a missile that can be used from a distance rather than an army that would fight hand to hand. It could also be a sanction or other means to conquer an enemy without engaging him in hand to hand combat.

The rider is given a crown. What does the crown mean? He is made a king or a leader of a nation. Who gave him the crown? It must be God. One of the four living creatures said come and " a crown was given to him". And," he went out conquering, and to conquer".

So, a careful reading of this verse tells us that Christ starts the end-times by breaking the first seal, a king or national leader is crowned by God and sent to conquer using weapons that he can use to conquer from a distance. We will talk more about this later.

3   And when He broke the second seal, I heard the second living creature saying, "Come."
4   And another, a <u>red horse</u>, went out; and to him who sat on it, it was granted to take peace from the earth, and that {men} should slay one another; and a great sword was given to him.

When Seal 2 is broken, a red horse goes out. He is allowed by God, "granted," to take peace from the earth, not a country or region, but the whole earth. He is given a great sword (means) so that <u>men shall slay one another</u>. This is not a war where nations invade nations. This clearly describes people killing each other up close and personal throughout the world. What would this look like? Perhaps this means suicide bombing and *other acts of terrorism. Note that the horse is red and that we learned in Chapter 12 that red is the color of the dragon/Satan.*

5   And when He broke the third seal, I heard the third living creature saying, "Come." And I looked, and behold, a <u>black horse</u>; and he who sat on it had a pair of scales in his hand.
6   And I heard as it were a voice in the center of the four living creatures saying, "A quart of wheat for a denarius, and three quarts of barley for a denarius; and do not harm the oil and the wine."

Seal 3 clearly describes economic collapse. The scales represent commerce in grain, oil, and wine, commodities that are the staples of John's day and ours. A denarius is the equivalent of a day's wage. So, this verse is saying that a person would have to work all day to earn enough to survive a day. Interesting that they should use the word oil. This could be an example of a word in the Bible sent to us down through the centuries so that we might have insight in the end-times. Oil in John's day probably meant olive oil or oil for lamps. Now when we think of oil we think of the world's primary source of energy.

7   And when He broke the fourth seal, I heard the voice of the fourth living creature saying, "Come."
8   And I looked, and behold, an <u>ashen horse</u>; and he who sat on it had the name Death; and Hades was following with him. And authority was given to them over a fourth of the earth, to kill with sword and with famine and with pestilence and by the wild beasts of the earth.

The forth seal shows the earth in turmoil and despair, men killing each other, famine, and pestilence. A fourth of the earth is sick and dying.

If we back up and look at the first four seals together, we get a picture of a sequence of events that occur on earth by people on the earth at the beginning of the end-times. These first four seals are not launching bands of angels to act on earth. I believe that the horses are the result of actions by people here on earth, both good and bad, that are acting according to God's prophecy.

If we look at the story of seals 1-4 we see a picture of a nation conquering for a noble purpose. This results in terrorists actions that take peace from the world, followed by economic collapse, followed by a forth of the earth sick and dying. At this point nations and communities would be at war with each other to protect their own interest. Does any of this sound familiar or possible?

Christ tells us through the Gospels that wars between nations and natural disasters are not the signal of the end. It is the events just described that are the signal that the end-times have begun. Lets see what Jesus says in the Gospels.

> Matt 24:6-8
> 6   "And you will be hearing of wars and rumors of wars; see that you are not frightened, for {those things} must take place, but {that} is not yet the end.
> 7   "For nation will rise against nation, and kingdom against kingdom, and in various places there will be famines and earthquakes.
> 8   "But all these things are {merely} the beginning of birth pangs.

> Mark 13:7-8
> 7   "And when you hear of wars and rumors of wars, do not be frightened; {those things} must take place; but {that is} not yet the end.
> 8   "For nation will arise against nation, and kingdom against kingdom; there will be earthquakes in various places;

there will {also} be famines. These things are {merely} the beginning of birth pangs.

Luke 21:9-11
9   "And when you hear of wars and disturbances, do not be terrified; for these things must take place first, but <u>the end {does} not {follow} immediately.</u>"
10   Then He continued by saying to them, "Nation will rise against nation, and kingdom against kingdom,
11   and there will be great earthquakes, and in various places plagues and famines; and there will be terrors and great signs from heaven.

Birth pangs will take place before the end-times. The Gospels specifically say that the end-times will not take place immediately following these events. In fact, wars between nations and natural disasters have taken place since the beginning of mankind. In all three Gospels, Christ is telling the disciples not to worry when they see such things, but they will increase in strength and frequency as we get closer to the end- times as birth pangs do. It is the events of the first four seals and what Jesus says next, as expanded by John in Revelation Chapter 6 that will give us the true signs to look for.

Tribulation#1 - Satan's Tribulation

9   And when He broke the fifth seal, I saw underneath the altar the souls of those who had been <u>slain</u> because of the word of God, and <u>because of the testimony which they had **maintained**</u>;
10   and they cried out with a loud voice, saying, "How long, O Lord, holy and true, wilt Thou refrain from judging and avenging our blood on those who dwell on the earth?"
11   And there was given to each of them a **white** robe; and they were told that they should rest for a little while longer, <u>until</u>

<u>{the number of} their fellow servants and their brethren who were to be killed even as they had been, should be completed also</u>.

The fifth seal is what is going on in heaven as Christians are being purged on earth. These are Christians that have been killed because they gave testimony of God. It also shows that God comforts them, but says that others must be killed as well. Once again God is rewarding Christians for their perseverance and is not intervening to stop the tribulation on earth. But what is going on on earth that is resulting in the deaths of the followers of God? I believe the answer lays in Chapters 13, 17, and the beginning of Chapter 11 "the tribulation of the beast". I call this Tribulation #1, because it is the first tribulation of the end-times. During this tribulation, Christians on earth suffer from the evil that Satan is imparting through the beast.

Lets learn more about what Satan is up to during this period. It becomes clear when you reorder Revelation to put Chapters 13, 17, and the beginning of Chapter 11 between Chapter 6 verses 11 and 12. These Chapters describe what is going on on earth during Seal 5 and before Seal 6.

Tribulation of the Beast

Rev 13:1-18
CHAPTER 13

1   And he stood on the sand of the seashore. And I saw a <u>beast</u> coming up out of the sea, having ten horns and seven heads, and on his horns {were} ten diadems, and on his heads {were} blasphemous names.
2   And the <u>beast</u> which I saw was like a leopard, and his feet were like {those} of a bear, and his mouth like the mouth of a lion. And the <u>dragon</u> gave him his power and his throne and great authority.

By seal 5 the earth is in anarchy and turmoil. Terrorism, fighting, hunger and disease are rampant. This is the opportunity that Satan has been waiting for. The people of the earth who are not Christians are looking for a savior. Satan, who is the dragon, raises up a leader, the beast (the Antichrist) for the world to rally around. This is the same beast described in Revelation Chapter 17 verse 3 because they both have the same number of heads and horns. The heads and horns are defined as kings. The seven heads of the beast are a progression of kingdoms over history and the 10 horns are 10 world leaders that will be giving power to the beast in the end-time. Nazi Germany is a relatively mild example of what will be the state of affairs. In the 1930's Germany was in economic despair. The Germans rallied behind a charismatic leader, and found a group of people to persecute, the Jews. This tribulation, however, will make Nazi Germany seem tame. If the sea symbolizes people and crowns / diadems are the symbols of a ruler, then this shows that the beast will be chosen by Satan from the leaders of the earth.

3   And {I saw} one of his heads <u>as if</u> it had been slain, and his fatal wound was healed. And the whole earth was amazed {and followed} after the <u>beast</u>;
4   and they worshiped the <u>dragon,</u> because he gave his authority to the <u>beast</u>; and they worshiped the <u>beast,</u> saying, "Who is like the <u>beast</u>, and <u>who is able to wage war with him?</u>"

The end of verse 4 shows that the people of the earth worship the beast because they think he can return peace and stability to the world ("<u>who is able to wage war with him?</u>). They are deceived.

> <u>2Th. 2:3</u> Don't let anyone **deceive** you in any way, for that day will not come until the <u>rebellion</u> occurs and the man of lawlessness is revealed, the man doomed to destruction.

Eph. 5:6 Let no one **deceive** you with empty words, for because of such things God's wrath comes on those who are disobedient.

Col. 2:4 I tell you this so that no one may **deceive** you by fine-sounding arguments.

5   And there was given to him a mouth speaking arrogant words and blasphemies; and authority to act for forty-two months was given to him.
6   And he opened his mouth in blasphemies against God, to blaspheme His name and His tabernacle, {that is} those who dwell in heaven.
7   And it was given to him to make <u>war with the saints and to overcome them;</u> and authority over <u>every</u> tribe and people and tongue and nation was given to him.
8   And all who dwell on the earth will worship him, {everyone} whose name has not been written from the foundation of the world in **the book of life** of the Lamb who has been slain.
9   If anyone has an ear, let him hear.
10   If anyone {is destined} for captivity, to captivity he goes; if anyone kills with the sword, with the sword he must be killed. Here is the **perseverance** and the faith of the saints.

The world will look to the beast to solve their problems and one of the problems is the Christians. Notice that this isn't just in a given country or in the Middle East. <u>Every tribe and people</u> will seek out and kill Christian saints. Notice too the reference to the Book of Life. This helps confirm the ordering of Revelation scenes and our definition of the seven-sealed scroll.

Life on Earth During Seal 5

Verse 9 above says, "If anyone has an ear, let him hear." Let him hear what? I believe that this is telling us to listen to what it says in the other parts of the Bible to hear what will happen during this time. I am going to break my line-by-line discussion of Revelation to present text from the Old and New Testaments that speak to what it will be like when the beast is in control prior to God's intervention. I will present these scriptures in their entirety so that you can see them as a whole. This will give you a flavor of what is happening on earth while the events described in Revelation Seal 5 are happening in Heaven. My previous discussions should give you new insights as you read these Bible verses. I will also insert a time prospective to them that I will discuss later as the reordered Revelation address these times. Many of the verses leap forward at the end of the discussion to the end of Revelation, but the initial focus is on the Seal 5 time in the end-time chronology. When the gospel quotes Jesus saying "My name" he is saying "Christians". Lets see what the Jesus has to say in the Bible about the Seal 5 time on earth.

Matt 24:3-36

3   And as He was sitting on the Mount of Olives, the disciples came to Him privately, saying, "Tell us, when will these things be, and what {will be} the sign of Your coming, and of the end of the age?"

4   And Jesus answered and said to them, "See to it that no one misleads you.

5   "For many will come in My name, saying, 'I am the Christ,' and will mislead many.

6   "And you will be hearing of wars and rumors of wars; see that you are not frightened, for {those things} must take place, but {that} is not yet the end.

7   "For nation will rise against nation, and kingdom against kingdom, and in various places there will be famines and earthquakes.

8   "But all these things are {merely} the beginning of birth pangs.

Here is where the gospel timeline moves from before the end-times to during the end-times Seal 5. This is true in all three gospels.

9   "Then they will deliver you to tribulation, and will kill you, and <u>you will be hated by all nations on account of My name.</u>

10   "And at that time many will fall away and will deliver up one another and hate one another.

11   "And many false prophets will arise, and will mislead many.

12   "And because lawlessness is increased, most people's love will grow cold.

13   "But the one who endures to the end, he shall be saved.

14   "And this gospel of the kingdom shall be preached in the whole world for a witness to all the nations, and then the end shall come.

15   "Therefore when you see the abomination of desolation which was spoken of through Daniel the prophet, standing in the holy place (let the reader understand),

16   then let those who are in Judea flee to the mountains;

17   let him who is on the housetop not go down to get the things out that are in his house;

18   and let him who is in the field not turn back to get his cloak.

19   "But woe to those who are with child and to those who nurse babes in those days!

20   "But pray that your flight may not be in the winter, or on a Sabbath;

21   for then there will be a great tribulation, such as has not occurred since the beginning of the world until now, nor ever shall.

22   "And unless those days had been cut short, no life would have been saved; but for the sake of the elect those days shall be cut short.

23   "Then if anyone says to you, 'Behold, here is the Christ,' or 'There {He is,'} do not believe {him.}

24   "For false Christs and false prophets will arise and will show great signs and wonders, so as to mislead, if possible, even the elect.

25   "Behold, I have told you in advance.

26   "If therefore they say to you, 'Behold, He is in the wilderness,' do not go forth, {or,} 'Behold, He is in the inner rooms,' do not believe {them.}

27   "For just as the lightning comes from the east, and flashes even to the west, so shall the coming of the Son of Man be.

28   "Wherever the corpse is, there the vultures will gather.

Here is where Seal 6 is broken. After the tribulation of Satan (Tribulation 1) then the sun will darken. The following verses describe what happens in Seal 6. This shows that there is more than one tribulation and that the timing break between Tribulation 1 and 2 is Seal 6. A more detailed description of the beast that inflicts the first tribulation on Christians and Jews is described in Revelation Chapter 17, as we will discuss shortly.

29   "But immediately after the tribulation of those days the sun will be darkened, and the moon will not give its light, and the stars will fall from the sky, and the powers of the heavens will be shaken,

At Trumpet 7

30   and then the sign of the Son of Man will appear in the sky, and then all the tribes of the earth will mourn, and they will see the Son of Man coming on the clouds of the sky with power and great glory.

31   "And He will send forth His angels with a great trumpet and they will gather together His elect from the four winds, from one end of the sky to the other.

32   "Now learn the parable from the fig tree: when its branch has already become tender, and puts forth its leaves, you know that summer is near;

33   even so you too, **when you see all these things**, recognize that He is near, {right} at the door.

34   "Truly I say to you, **this generation** (*i.e. one end-time generation*) will not pass away until all these things take place.

35   "Heaven and earth will pass away, but My <u>words</u> shall not pass away.

36   "But of that day and hour no one knows, not even the angels of heaven, nor the Son, but the Father alone.

Mark 13:3-32

3   And as He was sitting on the Mount of Olives opposite the temple, Peter and James and John and Andrew were questioning Him privately,

4   "Tell us, when will these things be, and what {will be} the sign when all these things are going to be fulfilled?"

5   And Jesus began to say to them, "See to it that no one misleads you.

6   "Many will come in My name, saying, 'I am {He!'} and will mislead many.

7   "And when you hear of wars and rumors of wars, do not be frightened; {those things} must take place; but {that is} not yet the end.

8   "For nation will arise against nation, and kingdom against kingdom; there will be earthquakes in various places; there will {also} be famines. These things are {merely} the beginning of birth pangs.

9   "But be on your guard; for they will deliver you to {the} courts, and you will be flogged in {the} synagogues, and you will stand before governors and kings for My sake, as a testimony to them.

10   "And the gospel must first be preached to all the nations.

11   "And when they arrest you and deliver you up, do not be anxious beforehand about what you are to say, but say whatever

is given you in that hour; for it is not you who speak, but {it is} the Holy Spirit.

Seal 5 is broken. As you can see above, Christians have been tested since the early church. At Seal 5 Christians are hated by the entire world. This and the abomination of desolation are the keys to Seal 5 timing.

12   "And brother will deliver brother to death, and a father {his} child; and children will rise up against parents and have them put to death.

13   "And <u>you will be hated by all on account of My name,</u> but the one who endures to the end, he shall be saved.

14   "But when you see the abomination of desolation standing where it should not be (let the reader understand), then let those who are in Judea flee to the mountains.

15   "And let him who is on the housetop not go down, or enter in, to get anything out of his house;

16   and let him who is in the field not turn back to get his cloak.

17   "But woe to those who are with child and to those who nurse babes in those days!

18   "But pray that it may not happen in the winter.

19   "For those days will be a {time of} tribulation such as has not occurred since the beginning of the creation which God created, until now, and never shall.

20   "And unless the Lord had shortened {those} days, no life would have been saved; but for the sake of the elect whom He chose, He shortened the days.

21   "And then if anyone says to you, 'Behold, here is the Christ'; or, 'Behold, {He is} there'; do not believe {him;}

22   for false Christs and false prophets will arise, and will show signs and wonders, in order, if possible, to lead the elect astray.

23   "But take heed; behold, I have told you everything in advance.

At Seal 6

24   "But in those days, <u>after that tribulation</u>, the sun will be darkened, and the moon will not give its light,

25   and the stars will be falling from heaven, and the powers that are in the heavens will be shaken.

At Trumpet 7

26   "And then they will see the Son of Man coming in clouds with great power and glory.

27   "And then He will send forth the angels, and will gather together His elect from the four winds, from the farthest end of the earth, to the farthest end of heaven.

28   "Now learn the parable from the fig tree: when its branch has already become tender, and puts forth its leaves, you know that summer is near.

29   "Even so, you too, **when you see these things happening**, recognize that He is near, {right} at the door.

30   "Truly I say to you, **this generation** will not pass away until all these things take place.

31   "Heaven and earth will pass away, but My words will not pass away.

32   "But of that day or hour no one knows, not even the angels in heaven, nor the Son, but the Father {alone.}

Luke 21:7-33

7   And they questioned Him, saying, "Teacher, when therefore will these things be? And what {will be} the sign when these things are about to take place?"

8   And He said, "See to it that you be not misled; for many will come in My name, saying, 'I am {He,'} and, 'The time is at hand'; do not go after them.

9   "And when you hear of wars and disturbances, do not be terrified; for these things must take place first, but the end {does} not {follow} immediately."

10   Then He continued by saying to them, "Nation will rise against nation, and kingdom against kingdom,

11   and there will be great earthquakes, and in various places plagues and famines; and there will be terrors and great signs from heaven.

12   "But before all these things, they will lay their hands on you and will persecute you, delivering you to the synagogues and prisons, bringing you before kings and governors for My name's sake.

13   "It will lead to an opportunity for your testimony.

14   "So make up your minds not to prepare beforehand to defend yourselves;

15   for I will give you utterance and wisdom which none of your opponents will be able to resist or refute.

At Seal 5

16   "But you will be delivered up even by parents and brothers and relatives and friends, and they will put {some} of you to death,

17   and <u>you will be hated by all on account of My name</u>.

18   "Yet not a hair of your head will perish.

19   "By your endurance you will gain your lives.

20   "But when you see Jerusalem surrounded by armies, then recognize that her desolation is at hand.

21   "Then let those who are in Judea flee to the mountains, and let those who are in the midst of the city depart, and let not those who are in the country enter the city;

22   because these are days of vengeance, in order that all things which are written may be fulfilled.

23   "Woe to those who are with child and to those who nurse babes in those days; for there will be great distress upon the land, and wrath to this people,

24   and they will fall by the edge of the sword, and will be led captive into all the nations; and Jerusalem will be trampled under foot by the Gentiles until the times of the Gentiles be fulfilled.

At Seal 6

25   "And there will be signs in sun and moon and stars, and upon the earth dismay among nations, in perplexity at the roaring of the sea and the waves,
26   men fainting from fear and the expectation of the things which are coming upon the world; for the powers of the heavens will be shaken.

At Trumpet 7

27   **"And then they will see the Son of Man coming in a cloud with power and great glory.**
28   **"But when these things begin to take place**, straighten up and lift up your heads, because your redemption is drawing near."
29   And He told them a parable: "Behold the fig tree and all the trees;
30   as soon as they put forth {leaves,} **you** see it and know for yourselves that summer is now near.
31   "Even so you, too, **when you see these things happening**, recognize that the kingdom of God is near.
32   "Truly I say to you, **this generation** will not pass away until all things take place.
33   "Heaven and earth will pass away, but My words will not pass away.

While Luke's description is slightly different from Matthew and Mark's, scholars believe that Luke had Mark's text when he wrote his. Mark's gospel is the earliest and probably most accurate. Perhaps Luke couldn't quite believe what Mark was saying. Revelation, written by John, however, does align with Mark's account.

Note that all three gospels say that the generation seeing the signs that Jesus is describing will see the end of it all. Since the *signs include the stars falling to earth and the Son of Man coming, this must be describing events in the future, the end-time events described in Revelation. The **you** Jesus is talking to is the end time generation.*

Since the Gospels speak of Daniel's prophecy lets see what it says. Chapter 11 in Daniel makes it clear that Daniel is speaking of the same end times and perhaps some of the same scenes that Christ shows John. This chapter describes the scene that is occurring on earth during the time when seal 5 is being opened in heaven. The reason we know this is because it describes the sequence of events that are happening on earth at the beginning of the end-times and prior to God's intervention. Note that the chapter begins with a statement that places these events "at the appointed time" which is the signal for the very beginning of the end-times.

```
Dan 11:29-45

CHAPTER 11
29   "At the appointed time he (beast) will
return and come into the South, but this
last time it will not turn out the way it
did before.
30   "For ships of Kittim will come against
him; therefore he will be disheartened, and
will return and become enraged at the holy
covenant and take action; so he will come
back and show regard for those who forsake
the holy covenant.
```

This describes the beast who is enraged with the holy covenant who are the believers of God. He sides with the nonbelievers.

```
31   "And forces from him will arise,
desecrate the sanctuary fortress, and do
away with the regular sacrifice. And they
will set up the abomination of desolation.
```

32   "And by smooth {words} he will turn to godlessness those who act wickedly toward the covenant, but the people who know their God will display strength and take action.
33   "And those who have insight among the people will give understanding to the many; yet they will fall by sword and by flame, by captivity and by plunder, for {many} days.
34   "Now when they fall they will be granted a little help, and many will join with them in hypocrisy.
35   "And some of those who have insight will fall, <u>in order to refine, purge, and make them pure</u>, **until the end time**; because {it is} still {to come} at the appointed time.

Here is where seal 5 is broken.

36   "Then the king will do as he pleases, and he will exalt and magnify himself above every god, and will speak monstrous things against the God of gods; and he will prosper until the indignation is finished, for that which is decreed will be done.
37   "And he will show no regard for the gods of his fathers or for the desire of women, nor will he show regard for any {other} god; for he will magnify himself above {them} all.
38   "But instead he will honor a god of fortresses, a god whom his fathers did not know; he will honor {him} with gold, silver, costly stones, and treasures.
39   "And he will take action against the strongest of fortresses with {the help of} a foreign god; he will give great honor to those who acknowledge {him,} and he will

cause them to rule over the many, and will parcel out land for a price.
40   "And at the end time the king of the South will collide with him, and the king of the North will storm against him with chariots, with horsemen, and with many ships; and he will enter countries, overflow {them,} and pass through.
41   "He will also enter the Beautiful Land, and many {countries} will fall; but these will be rescued out of his hand: Edom, Moab and the foremost of the sons of Ammon.

Notice that the beast will not hurt Edom, Moab and Ammon, where the Palestinian's and Jordanian's live today.

Notice too that he will overflow many countries. The term overflow in Daniel is similar to Revelation Chapter 12 Verse 15 "And the serpent poured water like a river out of his mouth after the woman, so that he might cause her to be swept away with the flood." *This is added proof from across the Bible that water and its affects are the symbol for people.*

42   "Then he will stretch out his hand against {other} countries, and the land of Egypt will not escape.
43   "But he will gain control over the hidden treasures of gold and silver, and over all the precious things of Egypt; and Libyans and Ethiopians {will follow} at his heels.
44   "But rumors from the East and from the North will disturb him, and he will go forth with great wrath to destroy and annihilate many.
45   "And he will pitch the tents of his royal pavilion between the seas and the

> beautiful Holy Mountain; yet he will come
> to his end, and no one will help him.

The Seal 5 time will be a terrible time as you can see. Now we return to the line-by-line discussion of Revelation Chapter 13 to see what else it has to say about this time.

The False Prophet

11 And I saw <u>another beast</u> coming up out of the earth; and he had two horns <u>like a lamb</u>, and he spoke as a <u>dragon.</u>
12 And he exercises all the authority of the <u>first beast</u> in his presence. And he makes the earth and those who dwell in it to worship the first beast, whose fatal wound was healed.

The second beast is the false prophet. This false prophet will look like Christ (lamb) but speaks like Satan (dragon). Remember the Gospel warning about false prophets that we just read.

13 And he performs great signs, so that he even makes fire come down out of heaven to the earth in the presence of men.
14 And he deceives those who dwell on the earth because of the signs which it was given him to perform in the presence of the beast, telling those who dwell on the earth to make an image to the beast who had the wound of the sword and has come to life.
15 And there was given to him to give breath to the image of the beast, that the image of the beast might even speak and cause as many as do not worship the image of the beast to be killed.

This idea of an image of a beast speaking must have sounded incredible when John wrote Revelation. Today such technology is ever present. Going back to the scholar's view of Revelation. Does this sound like a hidden message to the seven churches of

John's day or something that might be the result of today's technology.

16   And he causes all, the small and the great, and the rich and the poor, and the free men and the slaves, to be given a mark on their right hand, or on their forehead,

17   and {he provides} that <u>no one should be able to buy or to sell, except the one who has the mark, {either} the name of the beast or the number of his name.</u>

18   Here is wisdom. Let him who has understanding calculate the number of the beast, for the number is that of a man; and his number is six hundred and sixty-six.

You can ask almost anyone what the number 666 means and they will tell you it is the number of the devil. But, not many people are as familiar with the pervious verse that states that no one will be able to buy or sell without the number on his hand or forehead.

It is amazing that we have come to the point since the terrorist attacks of 9/11 that we have embraced security measures that would have been objectionable only a few years before. In the end-times as terrorism increases, the world economy collapses, and the beast arises, the world will turn to the beast to restore order. He will demand that there be a totally dependable way to identify people. Even without such events it seems reasonable today that people might want to have an EZ Pass type chip implanted under their skin to easily negotiate security lines and pay for items without fear of identity theft. Why carry a credit card if you could simply pass your hand over the terminal and have the bill sent to your bank. The beast simply makes this identification system global policy as part of the new economic system he puts in place to restore economic stability. By requiring each person to have a chip implanted in his or her body, it would be difficult to change from one identity to another. If the chip included a number issued only by the beast's government after swearing obedience to the beast he could not only implement his one world economic system, but also screen out Christians, Jews, and others who would not bow down to him. The world will welcome it.

The Answer to the Mystery of Babylon and the Harlot

Revelation Chapter 13 describes what it will be like on earth during the reign of the beast. But, how does the beast come to power? That is described in Chapter 17.

Rev 17:1-18
CHAPTER 17

1   And one of the seven angels who had the <u>seven bowls</u> came and spoke with me, saying, "Come here, I shall show you the judgment of the great harlot who sits on many waters,
2   with whom the kings of the earth committed {acts of} immorality, and those who dwell on the earth were made drunk with the wine of her immorality."

While the angel with the seven bowls doesn't pour the bowls on the earth until after the 7th trumpet, it is clear in Chapter 17 that John is actually talking to the angel during the beast's reign on earth prior to God's personal intervention. That places this text in the second Act of the reordered Revelation after Chapter 13 and before the end of Seal 6.

In this interlude, John sees a vision that gives us greater insight as to God's plan throughout history and what is happening on earth during Seal 5. This is where Revelation provides the definition of many of the symbols it uses in the prophecy: the woman, the harlot, and the beast who, together, perpetrate the first tribulation of the saints. It literally takes some reading across and between the lines to discover the true meanings.

3   And he carried me away in the Spirit into a wilderness; and I saw a woman sitting on a scarlet <u>beast</u>, full of blasphemous names, having seven heads and ten horns.

4   And the woman was clothed in purple and scarlet, and adorned with gold and precious stones and pearls, having in her hand a gold cup full of abominations and of the unclean things of her immorality,

5   and upon her forehead a name {was} written, <u>a mystery</u>, "BABYLON THE GREAT, THE MOTHER OF HARLOTS AND OF THE ABOMINATIONS OF THE EARTH."

6   And I saw the woman drunk with the blood of the saints, and with the blood of the witnesses of Jesus. And when I saw her, I wondered greatly.

7   And the angel said to me, "Why do you wonder? <u>I shall tell you the mystery of the woman</u> and of the <u>beast</u> that carries her, which has the seven heads and the ten horns.

8   "The <u>beast</u> that you saw was and is not, and is about to come up out of the abyss and to go to destruction. And those who dwell on the earth will wonder, whose name has not been written in the **book of life** from the foundation of the world, when they see the <u>beast,</u> that he was and is not and will come.

9   "Here is the mind which has wisdom. The <u>seven heads are seven mountains</u> on which the <u>woman</u> sits,

10   and they are <u>seven kings</u>; five have fallen, one is, the other has not yet come; and when he comes, he must remain a little while.

11   "And the beast which was and is not, is himself also an eighth, and is {one} of the seven, and he goes to destruction.

12   "And the ten horns which you saw are ten kings, who have not yet received a kingdom, but they receive authority as kings with the beast for one hour.

13   "These have one purpose and they give their power and authority to the beast.

14   "These will wage war against the Lamb, and the Lamb will overcome them, because He is Lord of lords and King of kings,

and <u>those who are with Him {are the} called and chosen and faithful.</u>"

15   And he said to me, "**The waters** which you saw where the harlot sits, **are peoples** and multitudes and nations and tongues.

16   "And the ten horns which you saw, and the beast, these will hate the harlot and will make her desolate and naked, and will eat her flesh and will burn her up with fire.

17   "For <u>God has put it in their hearts to execute His purpose</u> by having a common purpose, and by giving their kingdom to the <u>beast</u>, until the words of God should be fulfilled.

18   "And the <u>woman</u> whom you saw is the <u>great city</u>, which reigns over the kings of the earth."

Who is the woman?

In verse 5 above, it describes the woman as Babylon. In Verse 9, it talks about her sitting on seven mountains that refer to Rome. In Verse 18, it defines the woman as a great city, which reigns over the kings of the earth. Taken together, I believe that Verse 18 tells us who the woman is and unlocks the mystery. In Old Testament times the Babylonian Empire conquered the Jews and they were taken to Babylon in exile. Babylon was the "great city", the woman, of its day. During Daniel's time, Persia was the city. Later, in the New Testament, Rome (built on seven mountains) was the "great city" whose leaders crucified Jesus and killed the apostles. Babylon, Persia, and Rome were empires that ruled the entire known world at one time. I believe that the woman is, therefore, the great city at a time in history when a single empire rules the world; the world being what the Jews through whom God tells His story knows. Since this portion of prophecy is what happens in the end-times, we should look to identify the "great city" of that time as the place being addressed. The answer to the mystery is that the angel is describing what has happened when one empire rules the world. Revelation calls this city Babylon named after the great city that destroyed the first Temple in Jerusalem and exiled the Jews. There is further proof of this later.

Who is the harlot?

 Verse 5 then says that the great city is the "mother of harlots and of the abominations of the earth". The city isn't the harlot. The city gives birth to the harlot. So who or what is the harlot? I believe the harlot is the political and economic system at the heart of the city that controls the world. During the time of the original nation Israel, Babylon was the great city. The Babylonian Empire ruled initially by King Nebakenezer, the great king of that time, established the political and economic system of the empire. But, it was not only him that killed the prophets. It was the empire that he began. The economic and political system of the Babylonian Empire was the harlot. During John's day, Rome was the great city, the Caesars were the great kings, and the Roman Empire was the harlot. These cities ruled and had a system of trade that encompassed the entire known world. Abomination is defined as the taking the blood of the saints. The point made here is that throughout history the economic and political system of the great cities of the world, whether administered by kings or dictators, have been responsible for persecuting and killing the prophets and saints. These were rulers and political systems that set themselves up above God as Satan does. They killed God's messengers and bond servants when they ruled the earth. The city didn't kill the prophets; people did because of government politics and economic interests.

Who is the beast?

The beast is the same beast described in Chapter 13. He is the antichrist. You can tell that this is the same beast as described in Chapter 13 because it has the same number of heads and horns. He is the ruler of the great city during the end-times and implements the economic and political system that will kill the end-time saints. He is the person who steers the woman and the harlot during the end-times. Verse 8 foreshadows the fate of the beast. The beast will reign during Tribulation 1 and will be sent to the abyss at the end of Tribulation 3. He will then be raised from the abyss at the end of the millennium and then be destroyed. We will see this come to pass in future chapters.

What are the ten horns?

The ten horns are leaders of nations who will give their power to the beast. Notice that verse 12 says that they have not yet received a kingdom. This is the key to understanding that these leaders will come during the end-times prior to God's intervention not during John's time. This helps us place Chapter 17 here in the chronology.

Once again waters are peoples. Verse 15 provides the definition of the word water, seas, ocean, flood, etc throughout Revelation. If the harlot is the economic and political system, then this verse implies that this system covers the world.

So lets summarize. During the end-times there will be a great city, a political and economic system and a beast that will be raised up by Satan. Over the history of the world seven great kingdoms will be established that rule the world. They are collectively referred to as Babylon. This Chapter tells us that five of these world ruling kingdoms have existed up to the time of John, the sixth was alive then, the Roman Empire (seven mountains), and the seventh that will arise at the end-times, the beast's. In verse 13, we find out that the seventh king is returned to power after recovering from a fatal head wound. When he is returned to power he will rule the world as the eighth king establishing the seventh great city. He is the person responsible for Tribulation 1.

Notice that the beast hates the harlot not the city. It also says that the kings of the earth will destroy the harlot. I believe that the harlot referred to here is the political and economic system in existence as the end-times begin. In today's world that system is democracy and a market based economic system.

So, ten great kings of the earth will set the beast up in power and he will destroy the end-time economic and political system that had controlled the nations prior to his coming to power. Perhaps the beast doesn't like democracy and a free market driven economy. The beast will establish his great city and institute his economic system where you must have his mark to buy and sell. This is what is happening after Jesus Christ breaks the fifth seal.

Life of Nonbelievers During the Beast's Reign

Putting Chapters 13 and 17 before Chapter 11 makes what is happening in Chapter 11 more understandable. Chapter 13 describes what it will be like for believers. Chapter 17 describes what is happening from a big picture prospective. Chapter 11 describes what will it be like for nonbelievers living during this time in the last great city of the beast. The beginning of Chapter 11 of Revelation tells us that life for nonbelievers will return toward normal under the rule of the beast. Sure, the government is purging the people who do not worship the beast, but the economy is settling down and terrorist actions have stopped. In fact, all would seem well if it were not for the beast being plagued by witnesses of God that the beast cannot initially kill. Since God is acting through these messengers we can tell that Chapter 11 belongs in Act 2 of the reordered Revelation. God is still acting through people on the earth and as far as nonbelievers know, there is no god but the beast.

Rev 11:1-13

CHAPTER 11

1   And there was given me a measuring rod like a staff; and someone said, "Rise and measure the temple of God, and the altar, and those who worship in it.

2   "And leave out the court which is outside the temple, and do not measure it, for it has been given to the nations; and they will tread under foot the <u>holy city</u> for forty-two months.

3   "And I will grant {authority} to my two witnesses, and they will prophesy for twelve hundred and sixty days, clothed in sackcloth."

4   These are the two olive trees and the two lamp stands that stand before the Lord of the earth.

5   And if anyone desires to harm them, fire proceeds out of their mouth and devours their enemies; and if anyone would desire to harm them, in this manner he must be killed.

The holy city is Jerusalem. Who are the two witnesses? I cannot be sure, but I believe that they are Moses and Paul. Why do I think this? First, in Verse 4 the witnesses are described as olive trees. In Romans 11, verse 19-25, Paul describes Christian believers as wild olive branches that have been grafted into God's chosen people represented by an olive tree. In Romans Chapter 11, Paul tells us that the Old and New Testament covenants are connected and that Christian believers are made part of God's promises to the Jews. Who was the greatest old covenant witness for God, Moses. Who was the greatest New Testament witness, Paul.

Verse 4 above also describes the witnesses as lampstands. As we discussed before, lampstands are symbols of churches. Moses was the patriarch of the old covenant Jewish faith where Paul was the same for the gentiles. Together, I believe that the scripture is telling us that God's greatest witnesses from new and old covenants are brought back to life as these two witnesses. It would also make sense that these two prophets would have a special place at the Lord's throne. We saw earlier that the 24 elders on God's throne are the patriarchs of the twelve tribes of Israel and twelve apostles. Here we see the special place for the two men who established the foundation of synagogues and Christian churches.

We find further proof that the scripture is referring to Moses in the following verses where the powers of the two witnesses closely parallel the powers that Moses possessed to bring the Jews out of Egypt as described in Exodus Chapter 7.

6   These have the power to shut up the sky, in order that rain may not fall during the days of their prophesying; and they have power over the waters to turn them into blood, and to smite the earth with every plague, as often as they desire.
7   And when they have finished their testimony, the beast that comes up out of the abyss will make war with them, and overcome them and kill them.

This is the same beast that has set himself up as god that we have been talking about. Notice Verse 7 does not say that the beast comes up from the abyss to kill them. It says that it is the beast that comes up. He is the same beast that comes out of the abyss, but he has not gone there yet. This is another example of how one word changes the meaning, gives us a clue to the place this verse fits into the reordered Revelation, and shows us that there is really only one beast (other than the false prophet) described in Revelation.

8   And their dead bodies {will lie} in the street of the great city which mystically is called Sodom and Egypt, where also their Lord was crucified.

This Verse completes the mystery of the "great cities described in Revelation Chapter 17. In this verse we specifically told the final two of the six great cities that have existed up to the time of

John, Sodom and Egypt. This verse also says that the last great city will be Jerusalem (where Jesus was crucified). Therefore, the 7 heads of the beast are Sodom, Egypt, Babylon, Persia, Greece, Rome, and Jerusalem. The first 6 cities ruled the known world during their day, set themselves up above God, and killed God's prophets and saints. Sodom was the first great city during Abraham's time, Egypt during Moses' time, Babylon during the time of the first fall of Israel, Persia during Daniel's time, Greece the world superpower before Rome when Christ was crucified, and finally Jerusalem where the beast will establish his great city.

9   And those from the peoples and tribes and tongues and nations {will} look at their dead bodies for three and a half days, and will not permit their dead bodies to be laid in a tomb.
10   And those who dwell on the earth {will} rejoice over them and make merry; and they will send gifts to one another, because these two prophets tormented those who dwell on the earth.

The unbelievers who have the sign of the beast now believe that killing the Christians and Jews will be completed and that life will be good. The celebration of the killing of the witnesses sounds a lot like a Christmas celebration doesn't it. They are celebrating the end of Christ instead of his birth. But the celebration doesn't last long.

11   And after the three and a half days the breath of life from God came into them, and they stood on their feet; and great fear fell upon those who were beholding them.
12   And they heard a loud voice from heaven saying to them, "Come up here." And they went up into heaven in the cloud, and their enemies beheld them.
13   And in that hour there was a great earthquake, and a tenth of the city fell; and seven thousand people were killed in

the earthquake, and the rest were terrified and gave glory to the God of heaven.

Notice here that God makes one last ditch effort to warn the people of the earth that he is about to intervene. The witnesses warn the people of the beast's great city, and then God warns them by bringing the witnesses back to life and taking them to heaven. Then comes the earthquake. You will see in the next chapter that this earthquake begins God's intervention as Christ breaks seal 6. Verse 13's mention of an earthquake shows that Revelation Chapter 11 immediately precedes Chapter 6 verse 12 in our chronology.

Revelation Reordered

New
World
Rev. 21, 22
Millennium
Rev. Ch 20

God's Tribulation 3
Those That Remain
Rev. 11b, 15, 16, 19

God's Tribulation 2
Christians Still on Earth
Rev: 6b, 7, 8, 9a, 14, 10

End Times Begin - Tribulation 1
Tribulation of Beast
Rev: 4, 5, 6a, 13, 17, 11a

Before the End Times - Tribulation 0
Rev: 1, 2, 3, 12

Chapter 5. Act 3 - God Intervenes

By the beginning of Seal 6, the Beast seems to have everything going his way. Many of the Christians have been purged. The world is returning toward peace, the beast has set up his government, and most of the people of the earth are worshiping him and Satan. Then Christ breaks Seal 6 in Heaven. This is the beginning of Tribulation 2 when God begins to directly intercede while Christians are still on the earth. Read what the Gospels say below… the tribulation of those days (Tribulation 1) will end when the powers of the heavens will be shaken. The heavens are shaken during the second half of Chapter 6 when Christ opens Seal 6. This explains why Revelation Chapters 13 (focusing on believers), 17(big picture), and the first portion of Chapter 11(focusing on nonbelievers) precede seal 6 being opened in Verse 12 of Chapter 6. As I described earlier, the Gospels, containing Jesus words, are the means to help us to identify this sequence for reordering Revelation.

Matt 24:29
29   "But immediately after the tribulation of those days
(*Tribulation 1*) the sun will be darkened, and the moon will not give its light, and the stars will fall from the sky, and the powers of the heavens will be shaken,

Mark 13:24-25
24   "But in those days, <u>after that tribulation</u> *(Tribulation 1)*, the sun will be darkened, and the moon will not give its light,
25   and the stars will be falling from heaven, and the powers that are in the heavens will be shaken.

God Signals His Intent

Rev 6:12-17
12   And I looked when He broke the sixth seal, and there was a great earthquake; and the sun became black as sackcloth {made} of hair, and the whole moon became like blood;

This is the same earthquake that John described seeing in the great city after the two witnesses are taken to heaven in Verse 13 of Chapter 11. This shows that the first portion of Chapter 11 precedes this section of Chapter 6 and is describing the time when the beast is persecuting Christians and Jews.

13   and the stars of the sky fell to the earth, as a fig tree casts its unripe figs when shaken by a great wind.
14   And the sky was split apart like a scroll when it is rolled up; and every mountain and island were moved out of their places.
15   And the kings of the earth and the great men and the commanders and the rich and the strong and every slave and free man, hid themselves in the caves and among the rocks of the mountains;
16   and they said to the mountains and to the rocks, "Fall on us and hide us from the presence of Him who sits on the throne, and from the wrath of the Lamb;
17   for the great day of their wrath has come; and who is able to stand?"

I can't resist inserting a personal reflection into this portion of my discussion of the Revelation prophecy. At one time in my career

I was involved in aircraft accident investigations. In the conduct of an aircraft accident investigation the National Transportation Safety Board recovers the " Black Boxes" (which are actually orange) from the crash site. The black boxes are the flight data and cockpit voice recorders. As an accident investigation proceeds, flight data and voice recorders are transcribed and time sequenced so that the investigators can determine what was going on onboard the flight during the 30 minutes prior to the accident. An unofficial clue to the time when the pilots realize that the situation is beyond their control is when one of the pilots says " Oh Shit". These words appear in almost every fatal cockpit voice recording when the pilots begin to realize what is happening to them. Up to that point they are addressing the problems at hand. After that point, they begin to cry out. Revelation's description of Seal 6 is the "Oh Shit" moment for the unbelieving world.

Seal 6 is where the people of the earth who have followed the beast see that God is real, the Bible prophecy is true, and that they are doomed. Those believers who still live on earth, have persevered, and have not taken the sign of the beast begin to rejoice. The battle now is no longer between the followers of God and Satan who are on earth, but between the followers of Satan and God himself. Chapter 7 describes God's preparation of his earthly followers prior to beginning his tribulation, Tribulation 2.

God's Chosen Sealed

Rev 7:1-17
CHAPTER 7

1   After this I saw four angels standing at the four corners of the earth, holding back the four winds of the earth, so that no wind should blow on the earth or on the sea or on any tree.
2   And I saw another angel ascending from the rising of the sun, having the seal of the living God; and he cried out with a

loud voice to the four angels to whom it was granted to harm the earth and the sea,

3   saying, "Do not harm the earth or the sea or the trees, until we have **sealed the bond-servants of our God** on their foreheads."

4   And I heard the number **of those who were sealed**, one hundred and forty-four thousand sealed <u>from every tribe of the sons of Israel</u>:

We saw at the close of Revelation Chapter 6 that God is about to personally intervene to cut short Satan's tribulation (Tribulation 1) on behalf of God's Elect. He is about to unleash a terrible tribulation on the earth and He doesn't want his followers to be hurt by what He is about to do. Over the years, as I read Chapter 7 over and over I couldn't figure out why he would focus on 144,000 from Israel. I had always thought the Revelation was directed toward Christians and couldn't see why God would seal people from the tribes of Israel and not Christians. As I began writing this book and paying attention to the words used and the definitions from other parts of the Bible the scales fell from my eyes and I saw Verse 3 in a new way.

 God's first act, after signaling his intent, is to protect (seal) his bond servants, the Christians that have persevered through Satan's tribulation. He begins by sealing his bond-servants. As we discussed before, these are the Christian saints. This is to fulfill his prophecy in Revelation Chapter 3 Verses 10-13.

10   'Because you have kept the word of My perseverance, I also will keep you from the hour of testing, that {hour} which is about to come upon the whole world, to test those who dwell upon the earth.

11   'I am coming quickly; hold fast what you have, in order that no one take your crown.

12   'He who overcomes, I will make him a pillar in the temple of My God, and he will not go out from it anymore;

and I will write upon him the name of My God, and the name of the city of My God, the new Jerusalem, which comes down out of heaven from My God, and My new name.

13   'He who has an ear, let him hear what the Spirit says to the churches.'

He then seals the Jews he has selected to fulfill his covenant with Israel. Verse 4 can be misleading because it seems that the total number of people sealed is 144,000. But the previous verse says that bond-servants, i.e. Christians, are sealed then this verse says that he seals 144,000 from the tribe of Israel. I believe that he is saying two things in this verse; 1. That he heard the number of those who were sealed (which could have been millions) and 2. That 144,000 were from the tribe of Israel who were devout Jews. I believe that this is similar to the time of the Apostles. At that time many Jews became Christians, but others like Paul became Jewish zealots. Christ personally called Paul and in these end-times Christ will call 144,000 more. The following verses discuss Israel because here is where God completes his covenant with Israel.

5   from the tribe of Judah, twelve thousand {were} sealed, from the tribe of Reuben twelve thousand, from the tribe of Gad twelve thousand,
6   from the tribe of Asher twelve thousand, from the tribe of Naphtali twelve thousand, from the tribe of Manasseh twelve thousand,
7   from the tribe of Simeon twelve thousand, from the tribe of Levi twelve thousand, from the tribe of Issachar twelve thousand,
8   from the tribe of Zebulun twelve thousand, from the tribe of Joseph twelve thousand, from the tribe of Benjamin, twelve thousand {were} sealed.

Note here that the tribe of Dan is not mentioned and Manasseh one of Joseph's sons is. So Joseph's family gets two portions and Dan gets none. This is something that might be significant, but I do not yet know the answer.

Twelve thousand might also be a symbol for all that hear His call.

9   <u>After these things</u> I looked, and behold, a great multitude, which no one could count, from every nation and {all} tribes and peoples and tongues, standing before the throne and before the Lamb, clothed in **white** robes, and palm branches {were} in their hands;
10   and they cry out with a loud voice, saying, "Salvation to our God who sits on the throne, and to the Lamb."
11   And all the angels were standing around the throne and {around} the elders and the four living creatures; and they fell on their faces before the throne and worshiped God,
12   saying, "Amen, blessing and glory and wisdom and thanksgiving and honor and power and might, {be} to our God forever and ever. Amen."
13   And one of the elders answered, saying to me, "These who are clothed in the **white** robes, who are they, and from where have they come?"
14   And I said to him, "My lord, you know." And he said to me, "These are the <u>ones who come out of the great tribulation</u>, and they have washed their robes and made them **white** in the blood of the Lamb.

In verse 9 the scene shifts to heaven. It describes the fulfillment of the verses in seal 5 where God tells the saints to wait for the others who will be killed in the Tribulation 1 (of the beast). Notice they get white robes.

15   "For this reason, they are before the throne of God; and they serve Him day and night in His temple; and He who sits on the throne shall spread His tabernacle over them.
16   "They shall hunger no more, neither thirst anymore; neither shall the sun beat down on them, nor any heat;

17   for the Lamb in the center of the throne shall be their shepherd, and shall guide them to springs of the water of life; and God shall wipe every tear from their eyes."

From this point on, Christians have either been killed during Tribulation 1 and are in heaven before God or they are still on earth having been sealed by God to protect them from God's tribulation of those on the earth, Tribulation 2. Notice from a timing standpoint that Christ is still described as a lamb before the throne of God as he has been during the breaking of seals 1-6.

Let's summarize the prophecy of the Seals to this point. The seals describe the beginning of the end-times and the events between those who believe in God and those who are influenced by Satan. The Seals begin with a national leader setting out to do good, and a terrorist response that takes peace from the world. The result is economic collapse leading to disease and combat. The majority of the people of the earth embrace Satan who sets up his government, lead by the beast, to restore stability and purge the Christians and Jews. Ten kings support the beast becoming the absolute ruler of the world and they do away with the political and economic system that has been running the world. The beast establishes his great city in Jerusalem and persecutes and kills the Jews and Christians who will not worship him. Then God signals his intention to intervene. God seals his followers on earth and comforts his followers in heaven who have persevered and died during Satan's tribulation. Now it is time for God to begin to act. Seal 7 introduces the Trumpets, which will be Tribulation 2.

The Seventh Seal is Broken - The Book of Life is Opened

When Christ breaks the seventh seal the book of life is opened. This is followed by silence then trumpets. The trumpets herald

God's manifesting his power. Believers in heaven and on earth rejoice while those with the mark of the beast begin to hide.

Rev 8:1-13
CHAPTER 8

1   And when He broke the <u>seventh seal, there was silence in heaven</u> for about half an hour.
2   And I saw the seven angels who stand before God; and <u>seven trumpets</u> were given to them.
3   And another angel came and stood at the altar, holding a golden censer; and much incense was given to him, that he might add it to the prayers of all the saints upon the golden altar which was before the throne.
4   And the smoke of the incense, with the prayers of the saints, went up before God out of the angel's hand.
5   And the angel took the censer; and he filled it with the fire of the altar and threw it to the earth; and there followed peals of thunder and sounds and flashes of lightning and an earthquake.

The silence might indicate that God pauses to be sure that he should act because he know the seriousness of what he is about to do. The prayers of the saints convince him. Verse 5 above describes what causes the earthquake that we read about at the end of Revelation Chapter 6. Perhaps this censer refers to the stars that fall from the sky that Jesus described in the Gospels.

6   And the seven angels who had the seven trumpets prepared themselves to sound them.
7   And the <u>first</u> sounded, and there came hail and fire, mixed with blood, and they were thrown to the earth; and a third of the earth was burned up, and a third of the trees were burned up, and all the green grass was burned up.
8   And the <u>second</u> angel sounded, and {something} like a great mountain burning with fire was thrown into the sea; and a third of the sea became blood;

9   and a <u>third</u> of the creatures, which were in the sea and had life, died; and a third of the ships were destroyed.

10   And the third angel sounded, and a great star fell from heaven, burning like a torch, and it fell on a third of the rivers and on the springs of waters;

11   and the name of the star is called Wormwood; and a third of the waters became wormwood; and many men died from the waters, because they were made bitter.

12   And the <u>fourth</u> angel sounded, and a third of the sun and a third of the moon and a third of the stars were smitten, so that a third of them might be darkened and the day might not shine for a third of it, and the night in the same way.

Isn't this what Jesus foretold in Matthew 24:29 and Mark 13:24?

13   And I looked, and I heard an eagle flying in midheaven, saying with a loud voice, "<u>Woe, woe, woe,</u> to those who dwell on the earth, because of the remaining blasts of the trumpet of the three angels who are about to sound!"

Note that verse 13 says woe, woe, woe; one for each of the angels who will blow the final 3 trumpets. Revelation speaks of the last three trumpets as woes. These woes are a key to how to reorder Revelation from this point to the end of the trumpet tribulation, as I will show you.

Rev 9:1-12
CHAPTER 9

1   And the <u>fifth</u> angel sounded, and I saw a star from heaven which had fallen to the earth; and the key of the bottomless pit was given to him.

2   And he opened the bottomless pit; and smoke went up out of the pit, like the smoke of a great furnace; and the sun and the air were darkened by the smoke of the pit.

3   And out of the smoke came forth locusts upon the earth; and power was given them, as the scorpions of the earth have power.

4   And they were told that they should not hurt the grass of the earth, nor any green thing, nor any tree, but only the men who do not have the seal of God on their foreheads.

5   And they were not permitted to kill anyone, but to torment for five months; and their torment was like the torment of a scorpion when it stings a man.

6   And in those days men will seek death and will not find it; and they will long to die and death flees from them.

7   And the appearance of the locusts was like horses prepared for battle; and on their heads, as it were, crowns like gold, and their faces were like the faces of men.

8   And they had hair like the hair of women, and their teeth were like {the teeth} of lions.

9   And they had breastplates like breastplates of iron; and the sound of their wings was like the sound of chariots, of many horses rushing to battle.

10   And they have tails like scorpions, and stings; and in their tails is their power to hurt men for five months.

11   They have as king over them, the angel of the abyss; his name in Hebrew is Abaddon, and in the Greek he has the name Apollyon.

12   The first woe is past; behold, two woes are still coming after these things.

Note that this locust army is from God and answers to him. Everyone will be tortured unless they have the seal of God. People will be in agony yet see others who are sealed by God not affected.

At this point we break Chapter 9 to insert Chapter 18 in our reordered Revelation for the same reason Chapter 6 was broken to insert Chapters 13, 17, and the beginning of Chapter 11. How would I know to insert Chapter 18 in the middle of Chapter 9?

Let me explain the process I went through to discover this because it will give you some insight into how the scriptures opened up to me during my search for the right order.

I began by wondering how Chapters 17 and 18 fit into the chronology. They obviously both deal with the beast but they seemed like a side bar not a part of the chronology. It seemed logical that John would see them sequentially as a description of the beast and what would happen to him. I began by placing both chapters during seal 5. Chapter 17 fit, but 18 was talking about the destruction of Babylon by God at a time in the chronology before God began to intervene. It didn't make sense. Was it possible that these two chapters should be split? I then saw that Chapter 18 uses the words "Woe, woe" in Verses 10, 16, and 19. This does not occur any other place in Revelation. In many of my pilot training classes the instructor would stomp his foot to emphasize a point that was important. I thought that perhaps God is using Woe, woe as a "foot stomper" here to tell us where Chapter 18 fits into the text. Perhaps woe, woe is an indicator that the events described in this chapter take place near the time of the second woe. I then noticed that Chapter 18 starts with "After these things" which are also the same last words in Chapter 9 Verse 12 the end of the first woe. A clue to what goes together? But, more significantly, once I ordered the Chapters in this way, a startling thing became apparent; Chapter 9 is interrupted to allow Chapter 18 to describe what is happening on earth with the beast's great city between <u>Trumpet</u> 5 and 6 just as Chapter 6 was interrupted to identify the beast's great city between <u>Seal</u> 5 and 6. The beauty of this parallel tingled my spine. *This led me to the conclusion that I could order all of Revelation based on God's involvement with mankind and who was impacting whom. I realized that there are to be three Tribulations not one and discovered the true rationale for reordering Revelation. Chapter 18 describes what happens to the beast's great city when God begins Tribulation 2, so it fits chronologically into that section of the reordered Revelation. As* *a result of this reordering we now know that Chapter 18 shows the impact the Trumpet tribulations will have on the beast and his great city.*

Life on Earth as the Trumpets Blow

Rev 18:1-24
CHAPTER 18

1   <u>After these things</u> I saw another angel coming down from heaven, having great authority, and the earth was illumined with his glory.
2   And he cried out with a mighty voice, saying, "Fallen, fallen is Babylon the great! And she has become a dwelling place of demons and a prison of every unclean spirit, and a prison of every unclean and hateful bird.

This is the description of the judgment of the beast's "great city" and its economic and political system.

3   "For all the nations have drunk of the wine of the passion of her immorality, and the kings of the earth have committed {acts of} immorality with her, and the merchants of the earth have become rich by the wealth of her sensuality."
4   And I heard another voice from heaven, saying, "Come out of her, my people, that you may not participate in her sins and that you may not receive of her plagues;

So we can see that there are still God's people left on earth and some of them live in the great city of the beast. These are the people that have the seal of God. Notice also that God is calling his people out of the last great city, Jerusalem, just as he did with the first great city, Sodom before it is destroyed.

5   for her sins have piled up as high as heaven, and God has <u>remembered </u>her iniquities.

6   "Pay her back even as she has paid, and give back {to her} double according to her deeds; in the cup which she has mixed, mix twice as much for her.

7   "To the degree that she glorified herself and lived sensuously, to the same degree give her torment and mourning; for she says in her heart, 'I sit {as} a queen and I am not a widow, and will never see mourning.'

8   "For this reason in one day her plagues will come, pestilence and mourning and famine, and she will be burned up with fire; for the Lord God who judges her is strong.

9   "And the kings of the earth, who committed {acts of} immorality and lived sensuously with her, will weep and lament over her when they see the smoke of her burning,

10   standing at a distance because of the fear of her torment, saying, 'Woe, woe, the great city, Babylon, the strong city! For in one hour your judgment has come.'

Remember that Babylon is the name given to the great city of the day. Here it refers to the great city of the beast. In destroying this city, God remembers the sins of all the great cities including Babylon. Verse 10 also notes that the great city is a strong city. It becomes the superpower of the beast's time.

11   "And the merchants of the earth weep and mourn over her, because no one buys their cargoes any more;

12   cargoes of gold and silver and precious stones and pearls and fine linen and purple and silk and scarlet, and every {kind of} citron wood and every article of ivory and every article {made} from very costly wood and bronze and iron and marble,

13   and cinnamon and spice and incense and perfume and frankincense and wine and olive oil and fine flour and wheat and cattle and sheep, and {cargoes} of horses and chariots and slaves and human lives.

Note that slavery will become common once again. Human lives are also listed as commodities separately from slaves. With the

advance of science, who knows what that could mean? Perhaps clones used for replacement body parts.

14   "And the fruit you long for has gone from you, and all things that were luxurious and splendid have passed away from you and {men} will no longer find them.

15   "The merchants of these things, who became rich from her, will stand at a distance because of the fear of her torment, weeping and mourning,

16   saying, 'Woe, woe, the great city, she who was clothed in fine linen and purple and scarlet, and adorned with gold and precious stones and pearls;

17   for in one hour such great wealth has been laid waste!' And every shipmaster and every passenger and sailor, and as many as make their living by the sea, stood at a distance,

18   and were crying out as they saw the smoke of her burning, saying,' What {city} is like the great city? '

19   "And they threw dust on their heads and were crying out, weeping and mourning, saying, 'Woe, woe, the great city, in which all who had ships at sea became rich by her wealth, for in one hour she has been laid waste!'

20   "Rejoice over her, O heaven, and you saints and apostles and prophets, because God has pronounced judgment for you against her."

21   And a strong angel took up a stone like a great millstone and threw it into the sea, saying, "Thus will Babylon, the great city, be thrown down with violence, and will not be found any longer.

22   "And the sound of harpists and musicians and flute-players and trumpeters will not be heard in you any longer; and no craftsman of any craft will be found in you any longer; and the sound of a mill will not be heard in you any longer;

23   and the light of a lamp will not shine in you any longer; and the voice of the bridegroom and bride will not be heard in you any longer; for your merchants were the great men of the earth, because all the nations were deceived by your sorcery.

24   "And in her was found the blood of prophets and of saints and of all who have been slain on the earth."

Now it is time for the second woe.

Rev 9:13-21
CHAPTER 9 – Continued

13   And the <u>sixth</u> angel sounded, and I heard a voice from the four horns of the golden altar which is before God,
14   one saying to the sixth angel who had the trumpet, "Release the four angels who are bound at the great river Euphrates."
15   And the <u>four angels,</u> who had been prepared for the hour and day and month and year, <u>were released, so that they might kill a third of mankind.</u>
16   <u>And the number of the armies of the horsemen was two hundred million</u>; I heard the number of them.

This is not Armageddon. This is God's army. Read carefully. It is the angels who control these armies that have been prepared to deliver the three plagues for the 6th Trumpet. Believers are not hurt. Read below. The armies are not human.

17   And this is how I saw in the vision the horses and those who sat on them: {the riders} had breastplates {the color} of fire and of hyacinth and of brimstone; and the heads of the horses are like the heads of lions; and out of their mouths proceed fire and smoke and brimstone.
18   A third of mankind was killed by <u>these three plagues</u>, by the fire and the smoke and the brimstone, which proceeded out of their mouths.
19   For the power of the horses is in their mouths and in their tails; for their tails are like serpents and have heads; and with them they do harm.

20   And the <u>rest of mankind, who were not killed by these</u> <u>plagues, did not repent</u> of the works of their hands, so as not to worship demons, and the idols of gold and of silver and of brass and of stone and of wood, which can neither see nor hear nor walk;
21   and they did not repent of their murders nor of their sorceries nor of their immorality nor of their thefts.

Can you imagine the scene? The beast's great city is destroyed, plagues are ravaging the world, and now a 200 million man army shows up from God to cover the rest of the world. But, those not sealed by God still do not repent.

The Rapture of the Jews – Don't Be Deceived

Many Christians believe that God will bring believers directly to heaven without their dying at the beginning of the end-times so that they will avoid the tribulations. This has been called the rapture. We have come to the 6th trumpet and not yet seen any indication of the rapture in the end-time chronology. Up to this point the key word has been perseverance. Below in Chapter 14, we see the 144,000 Jews that were sealed by God meeting and rejoicing with Christ on Mount Zion. In the next verse they are in heaven. Revelation describes them as the first fruits. God has simply brought them to heaven. The first rapture, therefore, is the rapture of the Jews. This is a remarkable scene because it describes the Jewish survivors that have become Christians during Tribulation 2. They were persecuted as Jews during Tribulation 1 because they were faithful to Judaism and would not take the mark of the beast. Then God sealed them as Jews. Here they are with Christ knowing He is King of Kings and Lord of Lords. Their time on earth during the tribulations has shown them that Christ is their messiah and God's son. They are now to be with Him. Read this for yourself.

Rev 14:1-20
CHAPTER 14

1   And I looked, and behold, the Lamb {was} <u>standing on Mount Zion,</u> and with Him one hundred and forty-four thousand, having His name *(Christ)* and the name of His Father *(YHWH)* written on their foreheads.
2   And I heard a voice from <u>heaven,</u> like the sound of many waters and like the sound of loud thunder, and the voice which I heard {was} like {the sound} of harpists playing on their harps.
3   And they sang a new song before the throne and before the four living creatures and the elders; and no one could learn the song except the one hundred and forty-four thousand who had been purchased from the earth.
4   These are the ones who have not been defiled with women, for they have kept themselves chaste. These {are} the ones who follow the Lamb wherever He goes. These have been <u>purchased from among men as first fruits to God and to the Lamb.</u>
5   And no lie was found in their mouth; they are blameless.

I place Chapter 14 here because Verse 4 says that they are the first fruits. The Christians who have been sealed still remain, as you will see in Verse 12.

6   And I saw another angel flying in midheaven, having an eternal gospel to preach to those who live on the earth, and to every nation and tribe and tongue and people;

> Matt 24:14
> 14   "And this gospel of the kingdom shall be preached in the whole world for a witness to all the nations, and then the end shall come.

7   and he said with a loud voice, "Fear God, and give Him glory, because the hour of His judgment has come; and worship

Him who made the heaven and the earth and sea and springs of waters."

8   And another angel, a second one, followed, saying, "Fallen, fallen is Babylon the great, she who has made all the nations drink of the wine of the passion of her immorality."

Note that this is another clue that Chapter 18 must precede Chapter 14. Babylon falls as part of God's tribulation during Chapter 18 and here in the next reordered Chapter, 14, they are speaking of it having fallen.

9   And another angel, a third one, followed them, saying with a loud voice, "If anyone worships the <u>beast</u> and his image, and receives a mark on his forehead or upon his hand,

10   he also will drink of the wine of the wrath of God, which is mixed in full strength in the cup of His anger; and he will be tormented with fire and brimstone in the presence of the holy angels and in the presence of the Lamb.

11   "And the smoke of their torment goes up forever and ever; and they have no rest day and night, those who worship the <u>beast</u> and his image, and whoever receives the mark of his name."

12   Here is the **perseverance** of the saints who keep the commandments of God and their faith in Jesus.

So, while the Jews have come to believe in Christ and have gone to heaven with him, the Christians who have been sealed are still on earth and God is warning them to continue to persevere.

Let us say that you are a Christian, and you believe in the rapture, and you can't understand why you have had to go through the tribulation of the beast. And, then, you get the seal of God that protects you from God's plagues and you expect you will be called to heaven at any time. But, God's seal protects Christians from his tribulation, not the tribulation that continues to be imposed by the beast. Then, you see the Jews, who are also sealed by God, acknowledge Christ as their Messiah. And then, the Jews are raptured to heaven while your friends and family remain on earth. Would you begin to believe that God has forsaken you? Could you be deceived into turning away from God? Lets hear what God has to say.

13   And I heard a voice from heaven, saying, "Write, 'Blessed are the <u>dead who die in the Lord from now on!</u>'" "Yes," says the Spirit, "that they may rest from their labors, for their deeds follow with them."

This is the last test of the Christians that remain. The seal protects these Christians from God's plagues, but not from Satan's purges. Satan's followers have been preoccupied with God's plagues up to this point, but by now it is clear who the followers of God are (God's plagues do not touch them). The beast's last hope is to kill the remaining Christians in the hope that God will be defeated and his plagues will die with his followers. But God will not let this happen.

The Last Trumpet – Christ Returns

14   And I looked, and behold, a **white cloud**, and sitting on the <u>cloud {was} one like a son of man,</u> having a golden crown on His head, and a sharp sickle in His hand.
15   And another angel came out of the temple, crying out with a loud voice to Him who sat on the cloud, "Put in your sickle and reap, because the hour to reap has come, because the harvest of the earth is ripe."

Christ has opened the book of life and has become the King of Kings and Lord of Lords. Note that he is no longer shown as a lamb, but the son of man with a golden crown. He is now beginning to personally fight the beast and his followers. He first appears in the clouds and his followers on the earth will see him just prior to the seventh trumpet.

16   And He who sat on the cloud swung His sickle over the earth; and the earth was reaped.

17   And another angel came out of the temple, which is in heaven, and he also had a sharp sickle.

18   And another angel, the one who has power over fire, came out from the altar; and he called with a loud voice to him who had the sharp sickle, saying, "Put in your sharp sickle, and gather the clusters from the vine of the earth, because her grapes are ripe."

19   And the angel swung his sickle to the earth, and gathered {the clusters from} the vine of the earth, and threw them into the great wine press of the wrath of God.

20   And the wine press was trodden outside the city, and blood came out from the wine press, up to the horses' bridles, for a distance of two hundred miles.

Rev 10:1-11
CHAPTER 10

1   And I saw <u>another</u> strong angel coming down out of heaven, <u>clothed with a cloud</u>; and the rainbow was upon his head, and his face was like the sun, and his feet like pillars of fire;

This is a clue that Chapter 10 follows 14. This is <u>another</u> angel clothed with a cloud just as was Christ and another angel begin to act at the end of Chapter 14 above.

2   and he had in his hand a little book which was open. And he placed his right foot on the sea and his left on the land;

3   and he cried out with a loud voice, as when a lion roars; and when he had cried out, the seven peals of thunder uttered their voices.

4   And when the seven peals of thunder had spoken, I was about to write; and I heard a voice from heaven saying, "Seal up the things which the seven peals of thunder have spoken, and do not write them."
5   And the angel whom I saw standing on the sea and on the land lifted up his right hand to heaven,
6   and swore by Him who lives forever and ever, who created heaven and the things in it, and the earth and the things in it, and the sea and the things in it, that there shall be <u>delay no longer,</u>
7   but in the days of the voice of the <u>seventh angel, when he is about to sound, then the mystery of God is finished, as He preached to His servants the prophets.</u>

The rapture of the Christians is about to occur and Satan and the beast will be overthrown as the prophets predicted.

8   And the voice which I heard from heaven, {I heard} again speaking with me, and saying, "Go, take the book which is open in the hand of the angel who stands on the sea and on the land."
9   And I went to the angel, telling him to give me the little book. And he said to me, "Take it, and eat it; and it will make your stomach bitter, but in your mouth it will be sweet as honey."
10   And I took the little book out of the angel's hand and ate it, and it was in my mouth sweet as honey; and when I had eaten it, my stomach was made bitter.

It is hard to say but, perhaps the" little book" is the book of Revelation which gives us the wonderful understanding of God's great plan for believers and is, therefore, sweet. But, it also describes a horrific (bitter) time for Christians to experience while the tribulations are going on. Perseverance is the key.

11   And they said to me, "You must prophesy again concerning many peoples and nations and tongues and kings."

Revelation Reordered

New World
Rev. 21, 22
Millennium
Rev: Ch 20

God's Tribulation 3
Those That Remain
Rev: 11b, 15, 16, 19

God's Tribulation 2
Christians Still on Earth
Rev: 6b, 7, 8, 9a, 14, 10

End Times Begin - Tribulation 1
Tribulation of Beast
Rev: 4, 5, 6a, 13, 17, 11a

Before the End Times - Tribulation 0
Rev: 1, 2, 3, 12

Chapter 6. Act 4 - Tribulation of Those That Remain

Rapture of the Christians

At this point in the Revelation story, all those chosen by God whose names are in the book of life are in heaven except the Christian survivors of the beast's tribulations. They have seen the Jews saved and taken to heaven. They know, because they have read and understood Revelation that their time has now come to meet the Lord in the air.

Rev 11:14-19
CHAPTER 11

14 The second woe is past; behold, the third woe is coming quickly.
15   And the seventh angel sounded; and there arose loud voices in heaven, saying, "The kingdom of the world has become {the kingdom} of our Lord, and of His Christ; and He will reign forever and ever."
16   And the twenty-four elders, who sit on their thrones before God, fell on their faces and worshiped God,
17   saying, "We give Thee thanks, O Lord God, the Almighty, who art and who wast, because Thou hast taken Thy great power and hast begun to reign.
18   "And the nations were enraged, and Thy wrath came, and the time {came} for the dead to be judged, and {the time} to give

their reward to Thy bond-servants the prophets and to the saints and to those who fear Thy name, the small and the great, and to destroy those who destroy the earth."
19   And the temple of God which is in heaven was opened; and the ark of His covenant appeared in His temple, and there were flashes of lightning and sounds and peals of thunder and an earthquake and a great hailstorm.

At this point in the Revelation chronology, the angel sounds the 7ᵗʰ trumpet. As described in Verse 15, Christ takes his power and begins to reign. His first act is to claim his chosen from heaven and earth. This is best described in the following gospels and New Testament verses.

Matt 24:31
31   "And He will send forth His angels with a great <u>trumpet</u> and they will gather together His elect from the four winds, from one end of the sky to the other.

Mark 13:27
27   "And then He will send forth the angels, and will gather together His elect from the four winds, from the farthest end of the earth, to the farthest end of heaven.

But, Christians will finally be called to God. The Rapture of the Christians who have persevered on earth is about to take place. We know it is here in the Revelation story because God tells us when it will be.

1 Cor 15:51-57
51   Behold, I tell you a mystery; <u>we shall not all sleep, but we shall all be changed,</u>
52   in a moment, in the twinkling of an eye, **at the last trumpet;** for the trumpet will sound, and the dead will be raised imperishable, and we shall be changed.

53   For this perishable must put on the imperishable, and this mortal must put on immortality.

54   But when this perishable will have put on the imperishable, and this mortal will have put on immortality, then will come about the saying that is written, "Death is swallowed up in victory.

55   "O death, where is your victory? O death, where is your sting?"

56   The sting of death is sin, and the power of sin is the law;

57   but thanks be to God, who gives us the victory through our Lord Jesus Christ.

1 Thes 4:13-5:6

13   But we do not want you to be uninformed, brethren, about those who are asleep, that you may not grieve, as do the rest who have no hope.

14   For if we believe that Jesus died and rose again, even so God will bring with Him those who have fallen asleep in Jesus.

15   For this we say to you by the word of the Lord, that we who are alive, and remain until the coming of the Lord, shall not precede those who have fallen asleep.

These are the Christians that have died during the tribulation. Revelations 20:5 says that the other dead in Christ do not rise until after the millennium.

16   For the Lord Himself will descend from heaven with a shout, with the voice of {the} archangel, and with the trumpet of God; and the dead in Christ shall rise first.

This is the description of Revelation 11:15 above. All of those who have died in the tribulation and been given white robes from Seal 5 on are now alive with Christ.

17   Then we who are alive and remain shall be caught up together with them in the clouds to meet the Lord in the air, and thus we shall always be with the Lord.
18   Therefore comfort one another with these words.

So the Christians who are still on earth at the seventh trumpet meet Christ in the air along with all the saints that have died during the end-time tribulations. The people of the earth that remain will face the final tribulation; Tribulation 3, the seven bowls of wrath.

Christ Defeats the Beast

Rev 15:1-8
CHAPTER 15

1   And I saw another sign in heaven, great and marvelous, seven angels who had seven plagues, {which are} the last, because in them the wrath of God is finished.
2   And I saw, as it were, a sea of glass mixed with fire, and those who had come off victorious from the beast and from his image and from the number of his name, standing on the sea of glass, holding harps of God.
3   And they sang the song of Moses the bond-servant of God and the song of the Lamb, saying, "Great and marvelous are Thy works, O Lord God, the Almighty; Righteous and true are Thy ways, Thou King of the nations.

So here it is clearly stated. Both Jews, song of Moses, and Christians, song of the lamb, will be saved in the end and now there is no one left on earth that is chosen by God. They are standing on the sea of glass who, as we discussed before, are the people who have died prior to the end-times who have not yet been raised. They will rise after the millennium as stated in Chapter 20 Verse 5.

4   "Who will not fear, O Lord, and glorify Thy name? For Thou alone art holy; for all the nations will come and worship before Thee, for Thy righteous acts have been revealed."

5   <u>After these things</u> I looked, and the temple of the tabernacle of testimony in heaven was opened,

6   and the seven angels who had the seven plagues came out of the temple, clothed in linen, clean {and} bright, and girded around their breasts with golden girdles.

7   And one of the four living creatures gave to the seven angels seven golden bowls full of the wrath of God, who lives forever and ever.

8   And the temple was filled with smoke from the glory of God and from His power; and no one was able to enter the temple until the seven plagues of the seven angels were finished.

Here is what Tribulation 3 will be like. This tribulation will not touch God's saints for they will be in Heaven.

Rev 16:1-21
CHAPTER 16

1   And I heard a loud voice from the temple, saying to the seven angels, "Go and pour out the seven bowls of the wrath of God into the earth."

2   And the first {angel} went and poured out his bowl into the earth; and it became a loathsome and malignant sore upon the men who had the mark of the <u>beast</u> and who worshiped his image.

3   And the second {angel} poured out his bowl into the sea, and it became blood like {that} of a dead man; and every living thing in the sea died.

4   And the third {angel} poured out his bowl into the rivers and the springs of waters; and they became blood.

5　　And I heard the angel of the waters saying, "Righteous art Thou, who art and who wast, O Holy One, because Thou didst judge these things;

6　　for they poured out the blood of saints and prophets, and Thou hast given them blood to drink. They deserve it."

7　　And I heard the altar saying, "Yes, O Lord God, the Almighty, true and righteous are Thy judgments."

8　　And the fourth {angel} poured out his bowl upon the sun; and it was given to it to scorch men with fire.

9　　And men were scorched with fierce heat; and they blasphemed the name of God who has the power over these plagues; and they did not repent, so as to give Him glory.

10　　And the fifth {angel} poured out his bowl upon the throne of the <u>beast</u>; and his kingdom became darkened; and they gnawed their tongues because of pain,

11　　and they blasphemed the God of heaven because of their pains and their sores; and they did not repent of their deeds.

12　　And the sixth {angel} poured out his bowl upon the great river, the Euphrates; and its water was dried up, that the way might be prepared for the kings from the east.

13　　And I saw {coming} out of the mouth of the <u>dragon</u> and out of the mouth of the <u>beast</u> and out of the mouth of the <u>false prophet,</u> three unclean spirits like frogs;

14　　for they are spirits of demons, performing signs, which go out to the kings of the whole world, to gather them together for the war of the great day of God, the Almighty.

Note that there is no reference to believers, saints, or bond-servants in Chapter 16. The Christians and Jews are gone and now the beast and his followers know that they must defeat Christ. They prepare for the last great battle.

15　　("Behold, I am coming like a thief. Blessed is the one who stays awake and keeps his garments, lest he walk about naked and men see his shame.")

16   And they gathered them together to the place which in Hebrew is called Har-Magedon.

17   And the seventh {angel} poured out his bowl upon the air; and a loud voice came out of the temple from the throne, saying, "It is done."

18   And there were flashes of lightning and sounds and peals of thunder; and there was a great earthquake, such as there had not been since man came to be upon the earth, so great an earthquake {was it, and} so mighty.

19   And the great city was split into three parts, and the cities of the nations fell. **And** Babylon the great was remembered before God, to give her the cup of the wine of His fierce wrath.

20   And every island fled away, and the mountains were not found.

21   And huge hailstones, about one hundred pounds each, came down from heaven upon men; and men blasphemed God because of the plague of the hail, because its plague was extremely severe.

There is no real battle of Har-Magedon. The beast assembles his army there to do battle, but all that God does is have his angel pour a bowl into the air and say, "It is done". At this point the final plagues hit the earth. Then the world is turned over to Christ. Those with the mark of the beast don't stand a chance.

Notice that the great city and Babylon are mentioned separately. Here God is remembering all the "great cities" of the past as he pronounces his final judgment on the last great city during the end-time.

I also ask you to see that the three different tribulations I have identified to reorder Revelation align with the three divisions within the revelation itself; Tribulation 1 – Seals, Tribulation 2 – Trumpets and Woes, Tribulation 3 – Bowls of Wrath.

Christ and His End-Time Followers Become a Family

Rev 19:1-21
CHAPTER 19

1   <u>After these things</u> I heard, as it were, a loud voice of a great multitude in heaven, saying, "Hallelujah! Salvation and glory and power belong to our God;
2   because His judgments are true and righteous; for He has judged the great harlot who was corrupting the earth with her immorality, and He has avenged the blood of His <u>bond-servants</u> on her."

These are the voices of all the Christians that died or have been transformed during the tribulations. These are not the voices of all Christians that ever lived, as you will see shortly.

Chapter 19 follows Chapter 16 both in logical sequence and number sequence after Chapters 17 and 18 are moved forward. This helps us to know that the reordering of those chapters of Revelation are correct.

3   And a second time they said, "Hallelujah! Her smoke rises up forever and ever."
4   And the twenty-four elders and the four living creatures fell down and worshiped God who sits on the throne saying, "Amen. Hallelujah!"
5   And a voice came from the throne, saying, "Give praise to our God, all you His bond-servants, you who fear Him, the small and the great."
6   And I heard, as it were, the voice of a great **multitude** and <u>as the sound of many **waters**</u> and as the sound of mighty peals of thunder, saying, "Hallelujah! For the Lord our God, the Almighty, reigns.

7   "Let us rejoice and be glad and give the glory to Him, for the marriage of the Lamb has come and His bride has made herself ready."

This bride is Christ's church, all the Christians that lived and persevered during the tribulation.

8   And it was given to her to clothe herself in fine linen, bright {and} clean; for the <u>fine linen is the righteous acts of the saints</u>.

9   And he said to me, "Write, 'Blessed are those who are invited to the marriage supper of the Lamb.'" And he said to me, "These are true words of God."

10   And I fell at his feet to worship him. And he said to me, "Do not do that; I am a fellow servant of yours and your brethren who hold the testimony of Jesus; worship God. For the testimony of Jesus is the spirit of prophecy."

Why did John fall at Jesus' feet? Because he saw that this is what he would experience. Seeing this would certainly be overwhelming.

11   And I saw heaven opened; and behold, a **white horse**, and He who sat upon it {is} <u>called Faithful and True</u>; and in righteousness He judges and wages war.

12   And His eyes {are} a flame of fire, and upon His head {are} many diadems; and He has a name written {upon Him} which no one knows except Himself.

13   And {He is} clothed with a robe dipped in blood; and His name is called The Word of God.

14   And the armies which are in heaven, clothed in fine linen, **white** {and} clean, were following Him on **white horses**.

15   And from His mouth comes a sharp sword, so that with it He may smite the nations; and He will rule them with a rod of iron; and He treads the wine press of the fierce wrath of God, the Almighty.

16   And on His robe and on His thigh He has a name written, "KING OF KINGS, AND LORD OF LORDS."
17   And I saw an angel standing in the sun; and he cried out with a loud voice, saying to all the birds which fly in midheaven, "Come, assemble for the great supper of God;
18   in order that you may eat the flesh of kings and the flesh of commanders and the flesh of mighty men and the flesh of horses and of those who sit on them and the flesh of all men, both free men and slaves, and small and great."
19   And I saw the beast and the kings of the earth and their armies, assembled to make war against Him who sat upon the horse, and against His army.
20   And the beast was seized, and with him the false prophet who performed the signs in his presence, by which he deceived those who had received the mark of the beast and those who worshiped his image; these two were thrown alive into the lake of fire which burns with brimstone.

This is not a war. It is Christ seizing the beast and the false prophet and then taking over the world with his words.

21   And the rest were killed with the sword which came from the mouth of Him who sat upon the horse, and all the birds were filled with their flesh.

So to summarize the Third Tribulation, Heaven opens and the believers who have persevered on the earth during Tribulation 1 and 2 meet Christ in the air. This removes all believers from the earth. God then pours six of the bowls of wrath onto the earth. At that point Satan brings all his followers who are left on earth to Har-Magedon to fight Christ. God then pours the seventh bowl onto the earth and Christ rides out of Heaven with his army on white horses to claim the earth and throw the beast and false prophet into the lake of fire.

Chapter 7. Acts 5 - The Millennium

At this point in the Revelation story we are told when we will be raised to be with Jesus and learn what will happen during the thousand year reign of Jesus on earth, the millennium.

Two Resurrections

Rev 20:1-15
CHAPTER 20

1   And I saw an angel coming down from heaven, having the key of the abyss and a great chain in his hand.

2   And he laid hold of the <u>dragon,</u> the serpent of old, <u>who is the devil</u> and Satan, and bound him for a thousand years,

3   and threw him into the abyss, and shut {it} and sealed {it} over him, so that he should not deceive the nations any longer, until the thousand years were completed; <u>after these things </u>he must be released for a short time.

4   And I saw thrones, and they sat upon them, and judgment was given to them. And I {saw} the souls of those who had been <u>beheaded</u> because of the testimony of Jesus and because of the word of God, and those who had not worshiped the <u>beast </u>or his image, and had not received the mark upon their forehead and upon their hand; and they came to life and reigned with Christ for a thousand years.

So now we know how the beast will kill the Christians during the first tribulation. They will be beheaded. We also know that the believers during the tribulations will become Christ's family (his bride) and come to life again with him to rule during the millennium.

5   The rest of the dead did not come to life until the thousand years were completed. This is the first resurrection.

So Resurrection 1 is the resurrection of the end-time believers. Resurrection 2 will involve all the believers who died prior to the end-times.

6   Blessed and holy is the one who has a part in the first resurrection; over these the second death has no power, but they will be priests of God and of Christ and will reign with Him for a thousand years.

Those who come out of the tribulation will have the wonderful reward of reigning with Christ during the millennium.

7   And when the thousand years are completed, Satan will be released from his prison,
8   and will come out to deceive the nations which are in the four corners of the earth, Gog and Magog, to gather them together for the war; the number of them is like the sand of the seashore.

> Eph. 5:6 Let no one **deceive** you with empty words, for because of such things God's wrath comes on those who are disobedient.

> Col. 2:4 I tell you this so that no one may **deceive** you by fine-sounding arguments.

9   And they came up on the broad plain of the earth and surrounded the camp of the saints and the beloved city, and fire came down from heaven and devoured them.

10   And the devil who deceived them was thrown into the lake of fire and brimstone, where the <u>beast</u> and the false prophet are also; and they will be tormented day and night forever and ever.

Notice that this is not the battle of Har-Magedon *either. But, Satan continues to try the same methods to defeat Christ and some people on the earth who have been born during the 1000 years are still deceived by him in spite of the fact that Christ is personally ruling the world.*

At this point the prophecies of God are completed. The earth passes away. All the dead except those from the tribulation are judged. Those who died in Christ are raised to glory. Those who aren't face the second death.

Jesus Tells Us Where Heaven Is

11   And I saw a great **white** throne and Him who sat upon it, from whose presence earth and heaven fled away, and no place was found for them.

12   And I saw the dead, the great and the small, standing before the throne, and books were opened; and another book was opened, which is {the book} of life; and the dead were judged from the things which were written in the books, according to their deeds.

There deeds are their belief in God, their good works, and how they persevered over the tribulations they faced during their lifetime. I have termed their tribulation, Tribulation 0. The Christians that lived through the end-times, Tribulations 1 and 2, faced pressures that were unprecedented, so they have already been judged and married to Christ. Here, after the millennium, the spirits of the remainder of those who have died are brought before the throne of God to be judged.

13   And the <u>sea</u> gave up the dead which were in it, and <u>death and Hades</u> gave up the dead which were in them; and they were judged, every one {of them} according to their deeds.
14   And <u>death and Hades were thrown into the lake of fire</u>. This is the second death, the lake of fire.

Notice verse 14 only refers to death and Hades, not the sea.

15   And if anyone's name was not found written in the book of life, he was thrown into the lake of fire.

As I wrote this book, I pondered and prayed to understand Verse 13 -15 above for this is the key to what happens to those who die before the end-times prior to their being resurrected for judgment. Somehow this must be referring to Heaven and Hell. I could see that these verses tell us where people who have died before the end-times are prior to their being judged. But what are the sea, death and Hades. I had always assumed that this verse was simply saying everyone that had died. Then I saw it. There are two separate categories of places; 1. The sea, and 2. death and Hades. Read it again for yourself. I started to wonder why people who died at sea would be in a different category from people in death and Hades. I also wondered why death and Hades would be thrown into the lake of fire and not the sea as well. Then it came to me. The sea mentioned here is not the ocean. It is the sea of glass before the throne of God referenced in Revelation Chapter 4 Verse 6:

>Rev 4:6
>6   and before the throne {there was,} as it were, a <u>sea of glass</u> like crystal; and in the center and around the throne, four living creatures full of eyes in front and behind.

Once again water/seas mean people. I believe from this, that believers chosen by God who died before the end-times are in the sea of glass before the throne of God. The Sea of Glass is heaven. Others are dead or in Hades (Hell) until the earth passes away when their spirits are released. Christ holds the keys to death and Hades as stated in Revelation Chapter 1 Verse 18:

> Rev 1:18
> 18   and the living One; and I was dead, and behold, I am alive forevermore, and I have the keys of <u>death and of Hades.</u>

This verse is taken from Christ's description of who he is in John's Preamble. Notice that Christ does not say he has the keys to the sea. I conclude from this that the chosen of God go to heaven, which is the sea of glass before the throne of God. The names of those who are in the sea of glass are written in the book of life that Christ opens by breaking the seals during the end-times. Those who aren't in the book die and go to Hades. The sea of glass is before the throne of God and in a position to be in visual contact (glass) with God. While they rest from their earthly burdens, they will witness Christ breaking the seals and all that goes on in Heaven.

Once the spirits are released from the sea of glass, death and Hades, all are then judged. Those in the book of life will join Christ as the end-time believers already have. Those who are not in the book of life are dead and in Hades. They will be thrown in the lake of fire.

Blessed are those whose names are written in the book of life.

Chapter 8. Act 6 – The New World

Now we move to the final section of the reordered Revelation, the new world. This section is the end of the Revelation story and is in the same order that John saw it.

Rev 21:1-27
CHAPTER 21

1   And I saw a new heaven and a new earth; for the first heaven and the first earth passed away, and there is <u>no longer {any} sea.</u>

The sea of glass is now gone because all believers have been raised to live with Christ. Further proof that the sea in heaven is the sea described in Chapter 20.

2   And I saw the holy city, new Jerusalem, coming down out of heaven from God, made ready as a bride adorned for her husband.
3   And I heard a loud voice from the throne, saying, "Behold, the tabernacle of God is among men, and He shall dwell among them, and they shall be His people, and God Himself shall be among them,
4   and He shall wipe away every tear from their eyes; and there shall no longer be {any} death; there shall no longer be {any} mourning, or crying, or pain; the first things have passed away."

5   And He who sits on the throne said, "Behold, I am making all things new." And He said, "Write, for these words are faithful and true."

6   And He said to me, "It is done. I am the Alpha and the Omega, the beginning and the end. I will give to the one who thirsts from the spring of the water of life without cost.

7   "He who **overcomes** *(perseveres)* shall inherit these things, and I will be his God and he will be My son.

So everyone that ever lived, believed in God, and whose names are written in the book of life is alive with God and Christ in the new world. The others who have died and not believed are sent to the lake of fire and burnt up. They no longer exist. Notice that all those who's name are written in the book of life will become sons of God. The book of Hebrews tells us what it will be like when we are raised to live in the new world.

Heb 12:22-29

22   But you have come to Mount Zion and to the city of the living God, the heavenly Jerusalem, and to myriads of angels,

23   to the general assembly and church of the first-born who are enrolled in heaven, and to God, the Judge of all, and to the spirits of righteous men made perfect,

24   and to Jesus, the mediator of a new covenant, and to the sprinkled blood, which speaks better than {the blood} of Abel.

25   See to it that you do not refuse Him who is speaking. For if those did not escape when they refused him who warned {them} on earth, much less {shall} we {escape} who turn away from Him who {warns} from heaven.

26   And His voice shook the earth then, but now He has promised, saying," Yet once more I will shake not only the earth, but also the heaven."

27   And this {expression} "Yet once more," denotes the removing of those things which can be shaken, as of created things, in order that those things which cannot be shaken may remain.

28   Therefore, since we receive a kingdom which cannot be shaken, let us show gratitude, by which we may offer to God an acceptable service with reverence and awe;

29   for our God is a consuming fire.

8   "But for the cowardly and unbelieving and abominable and murderers and immoral persons and sorcerers and idolaters and all liars, their part {will be} in the lake that burns with fire and brimstone, which is the second death."

9   And one of the seven angels who had the seven bowls full of the seven last plagues, came and spoke with me, saying, "Come here, I shall show you the bride, the wife of the Lamb."

10   And he carried me away in the Spirit to a great and high mountain, and showed me the holy city, Jerusalem, coming down out of heaven from God,

11   having the glory of God. Her brilliance was like a very costly stone, as a stone of crystal-clear jasper.

12   It had a great and high wall, <u>with twelve gates</u>, and at the gates twelve angels; and <u>names {were} written on them, which are {those} of the twelve tribes of the sons of Israel</u>.

13   {There were} three gates on the east and three gates on the north and three gates on the south and three gates on the west.

14   And the wall of the city had twelve foundation stones, and on them {were} the twelve names of the <u>twelve apostles of the Lamb</u>.

From this I also believe that the twelve patriarchs of Israel and the twelve apostles are the twenty four elders before the throne of God.

Matt 19:28

28   And Jesus said to them, "Truly I say to you, that you who have followed Me, in the regeneration when the Son of Man will sit on His glorious throne, you also shall sit upon twelve thrones, judging the twelve tribes of Israel.

15   And the one who spoke with me had a gold measuring rod to measure the city, and its gates and its wall.

16   And the city is laid out as a square, and its length is as great as the width; and he measured the city with the rod, fifteen hundred miles; its length and width and height are equal.

17   And he measured its wall, seventy-two yards, {according to} <u>human measurements, which are {also} angelic</u> <u>{measurements.}</u>

18   And the material of the wall was jasper; and the city was pure gold, like clear glass.

19   The foundation stones of the city wall were adorned with every kind of precious stone. The first foundation stone was jasper; the second, sapphire; the third, chalcedony; the fourth, emerald;

20   the fifth, sardonyx; the sixth, sardius; the seventh, chrysolite; the eighth, beryl; the ninth, topaz; the tenth, chrysoprase; the eleventh, jacinth; the twelfth, amethyst.

21   And the twelve gates were twelve pearls; each one of the gates was a single pearl. And the street of the city was pure gold, like transparent glass.

22   And I saw no temple in it, for the Lord God, the Almighty, and the Lamb, are its temple.

23   And the city has no need of the sun or of the moon to shine upon it, for the glory of God has illumined it, and its lamp {is} the Lamb.

24   And the nations shall walk by its light, and the kings of the earth shall bring their glory into it.

25   And in the daytime (for there shall be no night there) its gates shall never be closed;

26   and they shall bring the glory and the honor of the nations into it;

27   and nothing unclean and no one who practices abomination and lying, shall ever come into it, but only those whose names are written in the Lamb's book of life.

Rev 22:1-21
CHAPTER 22

1   And he showed me a river of the water of life, clear as crystal, coming from the throne of God and of the Lamb,
2   in the middle of its street. And on either side of the river was the tree of life, bearing twelve {kinds of} fruit, yielding its fruit every month; and the leaves of the tree were for the healing of the nations.
3   And there shall no longer be any curse; and the throne of God and of the Lamb shall be in it, and His <u>bond-servants</u> shall serve Him;
4   and they shall see His face, and His name {shall be} on their foreheads.
5   And there shall no longer be {any} night; and they shall not have need of the light of a lamp nor the light of the sun, because the Lord God shall illumine them; and they shall reign forever and ever.

This is the beginning of the epilogue of the book of Revelation. It reiterates many of the thoughts written in the preface by John.

6   And he said to me, "These words are faithful and true"; and the Lord, the God of the spirits of the prophets, sent His angel to show to His <u>bond-servants</u> the things which must shortly take place.
7   "And behold, I am coming quickly. Blessed is he who heeds the words of the prophecy of this book."
8   And I, John, am the one who heard and saw these things. And when I heard and saw, I fell down to worship at the feet of the angel who showed me these things.
9   And he said to me, "Do not do that; I am a fellow servant of yours and of your brethren the prophets and of those who heed the words of this book; worship God."
10   And he said to me, "<u>Do not seal up the **words** of the prophecy of this book</u>, for the time is near.

11   "Let the one who does wrong, still do wrong; and let the one who is filthy, still be filthy; and let the one who is righteous, still practice righteousness; and let the one who is holy, still keep himself holy."

12   "Behold, I am coming quickly, and My reward {is} with Me, to render to **every man** according to what he has done.

Here Christ is telling John not to seal up what he saw and wrote. John didn't, but God did through the order of events he showed John. Then God is quoted by Christ.

13   "I am the Alpha and the Omega, the first and the last, the beginning and the end."

14   Blessed are those who wash their robes, that they may have the right to the tree of life, and may enter by the gates into the city.

15   Outside are the dogs and the sorcerers and the immoral persons and the murderers and the idolaters, and everyone who loves and practices lying.

Then Jesus Christ concludes his story to John.

16   "I, Jesus, have sent My angel to testify to you these things for the churches. I am the root and the offspring of David, the bright morning star."

17   And the Spirit and the bride say, "Come." And let the one who hears say, "Come." And let the one who is thirsty come; let the one who wishes take the water of life without cost.

18   I testify to everyone who hears the **words** of the prophecy of this book: if anyone adds to them, God shall add to him the plagues which are written in this book;

19   and if anyone takes away from the **words** of the book of this prophecy, God shall take away his part from the tree of life and from the holy city, which are written in this book.

20   He who testifies to these things says, "Yes, I am coming quickly." Amen. Come, Lord Jesus.

21   The grace of the Lord Jesus be with all. Amen.

Fore it is Jesus that reveals all things to us as individuals through the word and through His Spirit…. Including the book and interpretation of the Revelation.

Chapter 9. Are We the End-Time Generation?

What conclusions can we draw from the reordered Revelation? Where are we now in the Revelation story? These are the subjects of this chapter. In the preceding chapters, I have told you of my personal journey to discover what Jesus has put into the Bible to help us understand Revelation. I have described what Revelation has to say once it is reordered and pointed out things I thought you might want to consider while reading the verses. My hope is that as you read the preceding chapters, the Holy Spirit has spoken to you, brought you to a greater understanding, caused you to question what you might have heard previously, and brought you closer to God. These chapters are the most important part of this book because they contain God's words and offer his blessing.

In this chapter, I will put my case before you that we are in the end-times. I will put the reordered Revelation story into today's context because I believe that Christ is before the throne of God today and has already broken the first three seals. You decide.

God tells us that no one knows when the end will come, and I believe Him. However, God has also told us what to look for and told us that the generation that sees the signs He describes will see the end of it all. I believe that we are that generation.

> Mark 13:28-29
> 28   "Now learn the parable from the fig tree: when its branch has already become tender, and puts forth its leaves, you know that summer is near.
> 29   "Even so, you too, when you see these things happening, recognize that He is near, {right} at the door.

I will use the Gospel accounts to help interpret Revelation's meaning for us, but before I do this, I will discuss the seals. Jesus did not specifically mention in the Gospels the actions resulting from the first four seals being broken. The Gospels pick up the story at Seal 5. Perhaps the description of the events in the first four seals is a detail that Jesus knew that the disciples would not understand in their day. He did, however, show John so that he could write to the end-time generation in Revelation.

In Chapter 4 of this book, we discuss the seals. Lets begin by taking a closer look at the seals in today's context. By reordering Revelation we now understand the symbols of the dragon, the first and second beast, the "great city", the woman, and the harlot. By knowing who they are, we can get a better picture of what is going on on earth as the seals are broken by Christ in heaven. This then helps us to see what we might expect to encounter in the years ahead.

Are We the End-Time Generation: The Seals

<u>The First Seal</u>

Rev 6:1-2
1   And I saw when the Lamb broke one of the seven seals, and I heard one of the four living creatures saying as with a voice of thunder, "Come."
2   And I looked, and behold, a **white horse**, and he who sat on it had a bow; and a crown was given to him; and he went out conquering, and to conquer.

This is the first action in Heaven that Revelation says has an effect on earth and it should be the first sign to us that the end-times have begun. In Chapter 4, I show that we are talking about a white horse that is the color of purity and good in Revelation. I believe that the person riding the white horse is doing God's work on earth. Who is riding the white horse?

Many people have interpreted the rider as wars because of the word conquering, but I don't think so because wars are not good as implied by the term white. Others interpret the rider as Christ because Christ is riding a white horse in Revelation Chapter 19. I don't think so. The seals are situated in the chronology at the time before God directly intervenes in the world. We know that Christ is in Heaven before God's throne when He breaks the seals. If it was Christ who was riding out to conquer on the White Horse the conquering would be done and over; end of the Revelation story. This is a world leader or nation. I believe the white horse is the United States (U.S.).

But how could the rider of the white horse be the U.S.? We have previously identified six of the seven great cities that have ruled the world represented as the heads of the beast. The sixth head was the Roman Empire, which was the superpower of John's day. This is the first time since the Roman Empire that there has been a single nation that is the acknowledged world superpower; the U.S. But, could the U.S. be the seventh head of the beast? No, but we could be setting him up without knowing it.

Today, the economic and political system of the U.S. and much of the world is freedom, democracy, and a market based economy. Not a political and economic system that kills the prophets. This is why the rider is on a white horse. The U.S. is not conquering as all other nations have in the history of the world. The U.S. is conquering to spread freedom, democracy, and a market based system throughout the world. Notice the words of the prophecy say he is "conquering and to conquer". Conquer seems to imply military power where "to conquer" implies that actual conquering is not necessary. Doesn't this sound like what is happening today? The U.S. has recently literally conquered Afghanistan and Iraqi, but it has worked since WW II to spread freedom, democracy, and open markets for goods and services around the world. After WW II the U.S. gave up the territory it captured and worked to support the nations that suffered during the war, even the aggressors. We are still doing this today. The point made here is that throughout history the great cities and their political and economic systems, whether administered by kings or dictators, have been responsible for persecuting and killing the saints; performing abominations in God's terms. These kings have often set themselves up as a god. But, now the rider of the white horse is riding for God and freedom. The U.S. is not the great city or the harlot. It is trying to do God's work and it stands in the way of Satan and the beast. The beast must become greater than the U.S. to establish his kingdom.

To lend further credibility to the U.S. being the rider of the white horse, the rider is given a bow and a crown. This is the only place in the New Testament that a bow is mentioned. Why a bow when in most every other case in the Bible a sword is the weapon used to make the point? I believe that a bow is used because the person riding the white horse will strike from a distance as a bow and arrow would, as opposed to up close and personal when a sword is used. Clearly the U.S. has both long distance military weapons in the form of aircraft and missiles, which could be the bow to conquer. In addition, through the power of television, movies, the internet, international political bodies, economic sanctions, etc., the U.S. has worked to conquer the world by advocating free and democratic societies and open markets through means mainly other than weapons.

The rider is given a crown. What does the crown mean? It means ruler of a nation. While one could personalize the rider to be a specific U.S. President, I believe that the crown is given to the U.S. presidency not a person. Democracy and the election of presidents did not exist in John's time. The rider of the horses are clearly symbols, so the rider could be a person or a nation just as Babylon is a city and a nation. The U.S. has been "conquering" for democracy over many presidential administrations and it takes more than a president to wage war or conduct international policy. I, therefore, believe the rider is the U.S. not a given president. Who gave the U.S. the crown? It must be God. One of the four living creatures said come and " a crown was given to him". And," he went out conquering, and to conquer". It is easy to see that the U.S. has been blessed by God to become the greatest nation in the world at this time in history yet it has used its power to spread freedom and democracy not conquer other nations to make them part of an empire. This is unique in all of history.

So, my reading of the seal one verses tells us that Christ starts the end-times by breaking the first seal in heaven. The U.S. is raised up, crowned, by God and sent to bring freedom, democracy and a market economy to the world. If this is true, then Christ has already broken the first seal in heaven, perhaps as early as the end of WW II when the U.S. began it's climb to becoming the sole superpower. What is the result of U.S. actions?

The Second Seal

You need only open today's newspaper or watch TV to see the reaction of U.S. actions to bring freedom, democracy, and a market based economy to the world. Islamic radicals from the Middle East and around the world have declared war on the U.S. and anyone who does not believe as they do. The result is terrorism around the world including the attacks on the U.S. on September 11, 2001. Note that these attacks are not nation against nation. They are groups of individuals who will kill anyone, anywhere, at any time to make a point. They will even kill themselves in order to harm others in the belief that they are acting for their god. I believe that they have been deceived.

> Rev 6:3-4
> 3   And when He broke the second seal, I heard the second living creature saying, "Come."

4   And another, a <u>red horse</u>, went out; and to him who sat on it, it was granted to <u>take peace from the earth,</u> and that {men} should <u>slay one another</u>; and a great sword was given to him.

When Seal 2 is broken, a red horse goes out and he is allowed (granted) to take peace from the earth. He receives a great sword (means) so that men shall slay one another. This is not a war where nations invade nations. This is not talking about wars as they have been fought in the past. This clearly describes men killing each other up close and personal ("a great sword"), perhaps suicide bombing, beheadings, and other acts of terrorism. And this is not terrorism within a given country; it extends to "the earth". The world is no longer at peace because men are killing one another. The rider of the red horse is Islamic extremists.

I am reminded of a conversation I had with a senior aviation industry analyst on Wall Street about two years after the September 11 attack. She described how the U.S. won the cold war by outspending the Soviet Union in the arms race. This resulted in its downfall. She then noted that Osama Bin Ladin had invested about a million dollars to cause the U.S. over a trillion dollars worth of damage to its economy as a result of the September 11 attacks. The damage includes the costs of the attack itself, the economic impact due to transportation problems, lost sales, investment needed to increase homeland security, lost opportunity costs, the wars in Afghanistan and Iraq, etc. This is a lot of leverage in Wall Street terms. Then she said, "what if Osama had decided to invest a hundred million….we would be in a depression". Are the extremists raising the money as we speak? Will they eventually get weapons of mass destruction? Probably so.

So in the time of Seal 2 we see terrorism taking peace from the world as the U.S. continues trying to bring freedom and democracy to the world. Does this not describe what is happening today?

As the seals are broken, the full effects are not immediate, but build as birth pangs. The White Horse of the US has been riding for over 60 years. Terrorism has spread from inside countries to internationally for over 10 years. This is why I believe that Christ has within the last few years broken the second seal in heaven.

In 2012 the Middle East began going through a time of great unrest as a result of Arab people's desire for freedom and democracy. If we are in the end-time, terrorism will get worse in spite of the United States' best efforts to bring peace and democracy to the world. And, the attacks will come when we least expect it.

<u>The Third Seal</u>

If Seal 2 is already broken what does Revelation predict will happen next?

> Rev 6:5-6
> 5   And when He broke the third seal, I heard the third living creature saying, "Come." And I looked, and behold, a <u>black horse;</u> and he who sat on it had a pair of scales in his hand.
> 6   And I heard as it were a voice in the center of the four living creatures saying, "A quart of wheat for a denarius, and three quarts of barley for a denarius; and do not harm the oil and the wine."

Seal 3 clearly describes economic collapse and probably the collapse of the global market driven economy. The scales represent commerce in food, wheat, oil, and wine, the staples of John's day. A denarius is the equivalent of a day's wage. So, these verses are saying that a person would have to work all day to earn enough to survive for a day.

I first wrote this book in 2005 and it was published in 2007. At that time, terrorism was the major issue in the world. The housing bubble was still present and economic problems were the furthest thing from our minds. That is why I initially titled this chapter "Is the Red Horse Riding?". Since then, we have seen the world thrown into one economic crisis after another in the U.S., Europe, and around the world. Look at the U.S. housing and banking crises, and efforts to bail out countries banking systems to save the Euro. Who would have believed that global economic problems would follow terrorism so quickly on the global scene?

Economic turmoil signals the beginning of the collapse of the global society we enjoy today. This is what the terrorists are trying to achieve and what Revelation predicts.

I say, today, the Red Horse is riding and probably the Black Horse as well. The birth pangs have begun. Use this time to come close to God.

The Fourth Seal

Rev 6:7-8
7   And when He broke the fourth seal, I heard the voice of the fourth living creature saying, "Come."
8   And I looked, and behold, an <u>ashen horse</u>; and he who sat on it had the name <u>Death</u>; <u>and Hades</u> was following with him. And authority was given to them over a fourth of the earth, to kill with sword and with famine and with pestilence and by the wild beasts of the earth.

The forth seal shows that the results of first three seals escalate to where the people of the earth are in turmoil and despair.

People are killing each other and there is famine and pestilence. A fourth of the earth is sick and dying. I believe that this is describing the world in chaos resulting from terrorism, economic collapse and anarchy. Notice that Death is the rider and Hades follows behind. From our previous discussion we know that this means that many of the people killed will not be believers in God.

If we back up and look at the first four seals together, we get a picture of a sequence of events that occur on earth at the beginning of the end-times. These first four seals are not launching bands of angels to act on earth. I believe that the horses are actions by men here on earth, both good and bad, who are acting according to God's prophecy. If we look at the story of seals 1-4 with the U.S. as the White Horse that begins the events on earth, we see a picture of the U.S. as the global superpower spreading freedom, democracy, and a market driven society throughout the world. This results in terrorist actions that take peace from the world, and global economic collapse, followed by a forth of the earth sick and dying. At this point individuals, communities, and nations would be fighting with each other to protect their own interests. Does any of this sound possible? If this were to happen, people would look for a charismatic leader who could bring peace to the world. They just want things back the way they used to be. Most people would be happy to accept a charismatic global dictator as long as there was a promise that they would have peace and prosperity.

The Fifth Seal

By seal 5 the earth's turmoil has reached a peak. Terrorism and disease are rampant. This is the opportunity that Satan has been waiting for. The people of the earth who are not Christians are looking for a savior. They raise up a leader, the beast, the Antichrist, for the world to rally around.

Lets see again what Revelation Chapter 13 says.

Rev 13:1-7
CHAPTER 13

1   And he stood on the sand of the seashore. And I saw a <u>beast </u>coming up out of the sea, having ten horns and seven heads, and on his horns {were} ten diadems, and on his heads {were} blasphemous names.
2   And the <u>beast</u> which I saw was like a leopard, and his feet were like {those} of a bear, and his mouth like the mouth of a lion. And the <u>dragon</u> gave him his power and his throne and great authority.
3   And {I saw} one of his heads as if it had been slain, and his fatal wound was healed. And the whole earth was amazed {and followed} after the <u>beast</u>;
4   and they worshiped the <u>dragon</u>, because he gave his authority to the <u>beast</u>; and they worshiped the <u>beast</u>, saying, "Who is like the <u>beast,</u> and <u>who is able to wage war with him</u>?"
5   And there was given to him a mouth speaking arrogant words and blasphemies; and authority to act for forty-two months was given to him.
6   And he opened his mouth in blasphemies against God, to blaspheme His name and His tabernacle, {that is} those who dwell in heaven.
7   And it was given to him to make <u>war with the saints and to overcome them; and authority over every tribe and people and tongue and nation was given to him.</u>

People will be sure that the beast is the right leader to restore world order because he will appear to come back to life after receiving a fatal head wound. As in the case of Nazi Germany, the Anti-Christ will look for someone to blame for the problems with the world. Well, it is obviously the U.S. who started the whole mess by pushing freedom, democracy and a market driven economic system, and those Christians who were leading the charge. And besides, they won't worship the god of this world, the beast / Satan. The end of verse 4 above shows that the people of the earth will worship the beast because they think he can end the killing and return peace and stability to the world. Those who are not persevering Christians will be deceived.

The beast will return the world to what resembles a monarchy and once again play the harlot and kill the saints. Here, again, is how Revelation Chapter 17 puts it.

> 11   "And the <u>beast</u> which was and is not, is himself also an eighth, and is {one} of the seven, and he goes to destruction.
> 12   "And the ten horns which you saw are ten kings, who have not yet received a kingdom, but they receive authority as kings with the <u>beast</u> for one hour.
> 13   "These have one purpose and they give their power and authority to the <u>beast</u>.
> 14   "These will wage war against the Lamb, and the Lamb will overcome them, because He is Lord of lords and King of kings, and those who are with Him {are the} called and chosen and faithful."

This actually happens after Trumpet 7 when Christ Returns.

> 15   And he said to me, "The <u>waters</u> which you saw where the harlot sits, <u>are peoples and multitudes and nations and tongues</u>.
> 16   "And the ten horns which you saw, and the <u>beast,</u> these will hate the harlot and will make her desolate and naked, and will eat her flesh and will burn her up with fire.
> 17   "For <u>God has put it in their hearts to execute His purpose</u> by having a common purpose, and by giving their kingdom to the <u>beast</u>, until the words of God should be fulfilled.
> 18   "And the <u>woman</u> whom you saw is the great city, which reigns over the kings of the earth."

Notice from our discussion in Chapter 4 that from the beast's point of view the world economic system is the way to bring economic stability and achieve his ends, but from God's point of view this system is the harlot that kills the saints and worships Satan.

So, the beast will become leader of all the kings of the earth and will destroy (eat her flesh and will burn her up with fire) the U.S. inspired economic and political system that had controlled the world prior to the beast coming to power.

What will be the fate of the U.S.? I started by saying that the beast would have to become greater than the U.S., yet how would the beast be able to become greater than the greatest military power the world has ever seen? Perhaps that would be easy. If the terror and anarchy level was raised high enough and things got uncomfortable enough would the U.S. and other democracies vote to join the beast? Evidently so. Revelation says that the ten great kings will surrender their kingdoms to the beast. The beast will get their vote. Democracies will vote to become a monarchy of the beast. And the military might of the world will be under his authority.

The beast will establish his own great city, Jerusalem, based on an economic system where you must have his mark to buy and sell. By reordering Revelation the story flows absolutely logically to the point where God must intervene for the sake of the elect. Exactly as he said it would.

Are We the End-Time Generation: The Gospels

Lets look at what Jesus did tell us about the end-times in the Gospels. They contain three descriptions of Christ's answer to the same question asked by the disciples concerning how they will know when Christ will return and the end of the age will come. Each Gospel describes similar times, but adds different yet consistent details that are important to our knowing when we might expect the end-times to begin. I will highlight the key points and discuss how these points are fulfilled today. I will begin with Matthew and move on to Mark and Luke so you can get the picture across the gospels. Notice that John does not have a similar description, but he is chosen to write Revelation.

Matthew's Description of How We Will Know When the End-Times Begin.

Matt 24:3-25

3 And as He was sitting on the Mount of Olives, the disciples came to Him privately, saying, "Tell us, when will these things be, and what {will be} the sign of Your coming, and of the end of the age?"

4 And Jesus answered and said to them, "See to it that no one misleads you.

5 "For many will come in My name, saying, 'I am the Christ,' and will mislead many.

6 "And you will be hearing of wars and rumors of wars; see that you are not frightened, for {those things} must take place, but {that} is not yet the end.

7 "For nation will rise against nation, and kingdom against kingdom, and in various places there will be famines and earthquakes.

8 "But all these things are {merely} the beginning of birth pangs.

As you can see wars, famines and earthquakes are not the sign of the end, but they will increase in frequency and severity leading up to the end-times as birth pangs do.

9 "Then they will deliver you to tribulation, and will kill you, and you will be hated **by all nations on account of My name.**

Verse 9 is the key point. You know you are in the end-time tribulation when Christians (Christ's name) are hated by <u>all</u> nations and being killed. We are not there yet. This will happen at Seal 5 as I just described.

> 10   "And at that time many will fall away and will deliver up one another and hate one another.

They will fall away because they have been deceived and or do not persevere. During the reign of the beast it will the law to identify Christians and Jews to be purged as it was in Nazi Germany.

> 11   "And many false prophets will arise, and will mislead many.
> 12   "And because lawlessness is increased, most people's love will grow cold.
> 13   "But the one who endures to the end, he shall be saved.
> 14   "And <u>this gospel of the kingdom shall be preached in the whole world for a witness to all the nations, **and then the end shall come**.</u>

Verses 13 and 14 leap ahead to the end of revelation where the previous verses are describing what will happen during Seal 5. I don't believe that Verse 14 is the church spreading the gospel. This is talking about the end of times. It refers to God's angel announcing the gospel from heaven just prior to its end. See what Revelation 14: 6-7 has to say prior to the sounding of the 7th Trumpet:

> 6   And I saw another angel flying in midheaven, having an eternal gospel to preach to those who live on the earth, and to every nation and tribe and tongue and people;
> 7   and he said with a loud voice, "Fear God, and give Him glory, because the hour of His

judgment has come; and worship Him who made the heaven and the earth and sea and springs of waters."

So Verse 14 will be fulfilled just prior to the 7th Trumpet. Verse 15 now tells us of the beginning of the beast's reign during the end-times at Seal 5.

> 15 "Therefore <u>when you see the abomination of desolation which was spoken of through Daniel the prophet, standing in the holy place (let the reader understand),</u>

So lets see what Daniel has to say.

> Daniel 11: 31-33
> 31 "And forces from him will arise, <u>desecrate</u> the sanctuary fortress, and do away with the regular sacrifice. And they will set up the <u>abomination of desolation</u>.

Note here that Daniel, Verse 31 discusses two specific acts. First Satan's forces will desecrate the sanctuary fortress and do away with the regular sacrifice. The Babylonian and Roman Empires, which are both great cities of the past, did this. Then in the next sentence it talks about setting up the abomination of desolation. I believe there is a time break between these sentences that could be centuries in between. The temple was desecrated and the daily sacrifice was done away with when ancient Israel fell. The Dome of the Rock was built on the Holy site in 691 AD. We are still awaiting the abomination of desolation that will be set up in the end-times and the actions described in Verse 32 and beyond.

> 32 "And by smooth {words} he will <u>turn to godlessness</u> those who act wickedly toward the covenant, but the

> people who know their God will display
> strength and take action.
> 33   "And those who have insight among
> the people will give understanding to
> the many; <u>yet they will fall by sword
> and by flame, by captivity and by
> plunder, for {many} days</u>.

I conclude that the abomination of desolation is the beast establishing himself as god and killing the prophets, saints and believers as described in Matthew and Daniel as cited above. Where the beast is standing is the site where the holy of holies was in Solomon's temple in Jerusalem. This is a description of the beast beginning to act in his new great city, Jerusalem. How do we know it is Jerusalem? Matthew says so in the next verse.

> 16   then let those who are in Judea flee to the mountains;

The site of the holy place is confirmed by this reference to Judea and Luke plainly states Jerusalem in verse 21:15. Because we are talking of the end-times and the people of Judea are surrounded by armies and told to flee, then we must be talking about Israel. The exciting thing about this is that Israel exists today. This is a real world event that signals the beginning of the end-times. It was founded after WW II in 1948 by international agreement. This is the first time since the Roman Empire that Israel as a nation exists.

Given the preceding discussion, I believe that there are three indicators of the timing of the first seal being broken in Heaven.

1. The US begins its climb to world power to become the world's only superpower, the white horse,
2. Freedom and democracy defeated German and Japanese totalitarianism as a political force; this is the beginning of the conquering of the world by the U.S.

for democracy and a market based economic system. This was followed by the fall of the USSR. All of the USSR countries have also become Democracies, and,

3. Israel is established as a nation.

These three independent markers of Seal 1 all occurred at the end of WW II. I believe, therefore, that Seal 1 was broken by Christ in heaven in 1948.

Seal 2 begins with the rise of <u>global</u> terrorism. There have been terrorist attacks around the world for many years. I certainly cannot establish a specific date when seal 2 was broken in Heaven. However, I can say that terrorism took on a global scale and a global effort to fight terrorism was launched as a result of the attacks on the U.S. on September 11, 2001. This is why I believe that it is possible that Christ has recently broken Seal two. The Red Horse is riding.

Is the Seal 3 Black Horse riding? I am sorry to say, yes. I believe that we are now seeing the beginning of the effects. Here are some of the indicators:

- The global war on terrorism has weakened the global economies and the end is not in sight.
- The costs associated with natural disasters' such as the Japanese tsunami have reached monumental proportions.
- Individual investors are insecure because of market swings,
- Real estate value uncertainty threatening economic stability,
- High debt levels are rampant from individuals to nations,
- High unemployment rates are causing a crisis for those who want and need to work,
- Those who are unable to or don't want to work look to government to support them,

- Governments give benefits to their people that their nation, state, or locality cannot afford to sustain,
- Greed is rampant including banks and money managers who have undermined financial systems,
- The focus in society seems to be, "its all about me".

The global economic crisis will be followed by economic depression as the Black Horse rides. This will turn into global anarchy and death, which is Seal 4. Then comes Seal 5.

> 17   let him who is on the housetop not go down to get the things out that are in his house;
> 18   and let him who is in the field not turn back to get his cloak.
> 19   "But woe to those who are with child and to those who nurse babes in those days!
> 20   "But pray that your flight may not be in the winter, or on a Sabbath;
> 21   for then there will be a great tribulation, such as has not occurred since the beginning of the world until now, nor ever shall.
> 22   "And unless those days had been cut short, no life would have been saved; but for the sake of the elect those days shall be cut short.
> 23   "Then if anyone says to you, 'Behold, here is the Christ,' or 'There {He is,'} do not believe {him.}
> 24   "For false Christs and false prophets will arise and will show great signs and wonders, so as to mislead, if possible, even the elect.
> 25   "Behold, I have told you in advance.

Jesus does not specifically mention the first four seals in the Gospels as Revelation does. He describes what is not the sign of the end, he encourages his followers to prepare and to persevere through the trials that they will face prior to the end-times, and then He jumps to the beginning of Seal 5. His description from the beginning of Seal 5 on is consistent with the reordered Revelation story.

Looking at these verses in light of the reordered Revelation, you can see the dilemma the Jesus faced. His closest friends ask him for the sign that the temple will be torn down, his coming, and the end of the age as described in Matthew 24: 3 above. They want Him to reassure them that He is the Messiah and to explain to them how He will save Israel. He couldn't tell them that the end-times would be hundreds of years in the future and that He would return to save individuals not nations. Instead, He starts to tell them in a gentle way that the end will not come soon by saying that wars will not signal it and the gospel needs to be preached to the entire world. Preaching the gospel becomes His charge to them. He knows that they will be persecuted because of His name in their own time, so He wants to prepare them. Then he tells them of the true sign that the end is near, the abomination of desolation that is described by Daniel that will be fulfilled when he breaks Seal 5 in Heaven.

There is no reason to tell his disciples in detail the prophecy of the first four seals of Revelation because it is not pertinent to them. In fact he does not give the Revelation prophecy to John until after most of Jesus' apostles had been martyred. He does tell John to write the prophecy of the first four seals into Revelation for following generations to read because it is essential for us to know. In the Gospels He tells us how we will know when the beasts tribulation will begin.

Lets see how Mark describes Jesus' response to the disciples.

Mark's Description of How We Will Know When the End-Times Begin.

Mark 13:4-32

4   "Tell us, when will these things be, and what {will be} the sign when all these things are going to be fulfilled?"

5   And Jesus began to say to them, "See to it that no one misleads you.

6   "Many will come in My name, saying, 'I am {He!'} and will mislead many.

7   "And when you hear of wars and rumors of wars, do not be frightened; {those things} must take place; but {that is} not yet the end.

8   "For nation will arise against nation, and kingdom against kingdom; there will be earthquakes in various places; there will {also} be famines. These things are {merely} the beginning of birth pangs.

9   "But be on your guard; for they will deliver you to {the} courts, and you will be flogged in {the} synagogues, and you will stand before governors and kings for My sake, as a testimony to them.

10   "And the gospel must first be preached to all the nations.

11   "And when they arrest you and deliver you up, do not be anxious beforehand about what you are to say, but say whatever is given you in that hour; for it is not you who speak, but {it is} the Holy Spirit.

12   "And brother will deliver brother to death, and a father {his} child; and children will rise up against parents and have them put to death.

13   "And you will be **hated by all** on account of **My name**, but the one who **endures** to the end, he shall be saved.

14   "But when you see the abomination of desolation standing where it should not be (let the reader understand), then let those who are in Judea flee to the mountains.

Notice how closely Matthew and Mark agree to what will go on. The scripture makes a distinction between what will happen up to the end-times (birth pangs) and what will happen after. The abomination of desolation is the sure action on earth that will signal believers to run and hide. We know from the reordered Revelation that this is when the beast establishes his great city in Jerusalem.

By Seal 4 the world is in turmoil. Believers and non-believers are fighting to survive. Believers know what is happening and are looking for Christ to appear. Non-believers are looking for a leader to restore order. Satan, the dragon, raises up the beast from the world leaders by bringing him back to life after he receives a fatal head blow. I believe that he takes the throne at the holy of holies as god on earth while Christ is opening Seal Five in Heaven. The beast then turns the entire world against the Christians and Jews and begins to persecute and kill them. Read it for yourself below.

15   "And let him who is on the housetop not go down, or enter in, to get anything out of his house;
16   and let him who is in the field not turn back to get his cloak.
17   "But woe to those who are with child and to those who nurse babes in those days!
18   "But pray that it may not happen in the winter.
19   "For those days will be a {time of} tribulation such as has not occurred since the beginning of the creation which God created, until now, and never shall.
20   "And unless the Lord had shortened {those} days, no life would have been saved; but for the sake of the elect whom He chose, He shortened the days.
21   "And then if anyone says to you, 'Behold, here is the Christ'; or, 'Behold, {He is} there'; do not believe {him;}

22   for false Christs and false prophets will arise, and will show signs and wonders, in order, if possible, to lead the elect astray.

23   "But take heed; behold, I have told you everything in advance.

24   "But in those days, <u>after that tribulation</u>, the sun will be darkened, and the moon will not give its light,

This is the sign of Seal 6.

25   and the stars will be falling from heaven, and the powers that are in the heavens will be shaken.

Here the Gospel jumps to Trumpet 7.

26   "And then they will see the Son of Man coming in clouds with great power and glory.

27   "And then He will send forth the angels, and will gather together His elect from the four winds, from the farthest end of the earth, to the farthest end of heaven.

28   <u>"Now learn the parable from the fig tree: when its branch has already become tender, and puts forth its leaves, you know that summer is near.</u>

29   <u>"Even so, you too, when you see these things happening, recognize that He is near, {right} at the door.</u>

These verses have been viewed as the beginning of the tribulation, but they are not. These are the things that will tell Christians that are alive and sealed during the tribulation when to expect Christ to come, at the last trumpet. Notice that the sequence of events described here is consistent with the reordered Revelation.

30   "Truly I say to you, <u>this generation</u> will not pass away until all these things take place.

To me this is the most important clue for you and me concerning the timing of the end-times. I believe the "this generation" referred to here are the people who were born when Seal 1 was broken and will see the things Jesus describes in the gospels. All these things start with the rise of the U.S., the fall of totalitarianism to democracy, and the re-creation of Israel, and continue to the time when Christ appears at trumpet 7. That means that if you were born after 1948, then these Gospel verses and Revelation are specifically talking to you.

> 31 "Heaven and earth will pass away, but My words will not pass away.
> 32 "But of that day or hour no one knows, not even the angels in heaven, nor the Son, but the Father {alone.}

Luke's Description of How We Will Know When the End Times Begin.

Luke 21:7-35
7 And they questioned Him, saying, "Teacher, when therefore will these things be? And what {will be} the sign when these things are about to take place?"
8 And He said, "See to it that you be not misled; for many will come in My name, saying, 'I am {He,'} and, 'The time is at hand'; do not go after them.
9 "And when you hear of wars and disturbances, do not be terrified; for these things must take place first, but the end {does} not {follow} immediately."
10 Then He continued by saying to them, "Nation will rise against nation, and kingdom against kingdom,
11 and there will be great earthquakes, and in various places plagues and famines; and there will be terrors and great signs from heaven.

A point to note here is that both Matthew and Mark speak first of wars and natural forces including earthquakes and famine as birth pangs that precede the end-times then jump to what will happen at the end. Here, Luke reverses the order by talking about what will happen at the end and then says "before all these things". Even the gospels change the order of the description of the end times.

12   "But before all these things, they will lay their hands on you and will persecute you, delivering you to the synagogues and prisons, bringing you before kings and governors for My name's sake.

13   "It will lead to an opportunity for your testimony.

14   "So make up your minds not to prepare beforehand to defend yourselves;

15   for I will give you utterance and wisdom which none of your opponents will be able to resist or refute.

16   "But you will be delivered up even by parents and brothers and relatives and friends, and they will put {some} of you to death,

17   and you will be **hated by all on account of My name**.

The common statement between all three gospels is "hated by all". Christians have not been persecuted around the world since the Roman Empire. This verse cannot refer to the Jews, because it says specifically that those persecuted will be called by Christ's name; Christians. So, we know that Christians being delivered up to death in each gospel is the same indicator of Tribulation 1 of the beast. This will begin when the abomination of desolation stands.

18   "Yet not a hair of your head will perish.

19   "By your endurance (perseverance) you will gain your lives.

20   "But when you see Jerusalem surrounded by armies, then recognize that her desolation is at hand.

Is there anyone who doesn't know that Jerusalem is surrounded by armies today? This could not be true until Israel was reestablished as a nation. It is clear from this verse that Jerusalem surrounded by armies is a sign of the end-times. Here we also see the specific word desolation referring to Jerusalem or the nation of Israel. So to me the abomination of desolation referred to in Matthew and Mark are explained here in Luke.

Luke is telling us that armies will attack Jerusalem as part of the tribulation. Matthew and Mark are saying that the attacker will stand at the spot of the Jewish Holy of Holies in Jerusalem. What is standing there now? A Moslem mosque. According to Islamic tradition, this spot is also where Muhammad ascended to Heaven to be instructed by God. I believe that during the chaos of economic collapse during Seal 4, a charismatic leader, the beast, will rise at the beginning of Seal 5. Because he recovers from a fatal head wound, the world will worship him. He will then rally the world and attack Israel. The beast will then take his throne at the Dome of the Rock. That is the signal that the slaughter of Jews and Christians around the world will begin.

Many have written that Israel needs to reestablish their temple in Jerusalem before the end-times come. I think the daily sacrifice ended centuries ago and that the current Dome of the Rock is waiting to receive the beast.

> 21   "Then let those who are in Judea flee to the mountains, and let those who are in the midst of the city depart, and let not those who are in the country enter the city;
> 22   because these are days of vengeance, in order that all things which are written may be fulfilled.
> 23   "Woe to those who are with child and to those who nurse babes in those days; for there will be great distress upon the land, and wrath to this people,

24   and they will fall by the edge of the sword, and will be led captive into <u>all the nations;</u> and Jerusalem will be trampled under foot by the Gentiles <u>until the times of the Gentiles be fulfilled.</u>

Remember a Gentile is anyone other than a Jew. This is describing what will take place when the beast and those who have the mark of the beast control the world. This will continue around the world until the "O Shit" moment I described earlier when God signals his personal intervention at Seal 6. This is how Luke says it.

25   "And there will be signs in sun and moon and stars, and upon the earth dismay among nations, in perplexity at the roaring of the sea and the waves,
26   men fainting from fear and the expectation of the things which are coming upon the world; for the powers of the heavens will be shaken.
27   "<u>And then</u> (*at trumpet 7*) they will see the Son of Man coming in a cloud with power and great glory.
28   "But when these things begin to take place, straighten up and lift up your heads, because your redemption is drawing near."
29   And He told them a parable: "Behold the fig tree and all the trees;
30   as soon as they put forth {leaves,} you see it and know for yourselves that summer is now near.
31   "Even so you, too, when you see these things happening, recognize that the <u>kingdom of God is near</u>.
32   "Truly I say to you, <u>this generation will not pass away until all things take place.</u>

I.e. This will all happen within one generation. The generation born when Seal 1 was broken at the end of WW II. The baby boomers are the generation that will see the end of it all.

33   "Heaven and earth will pass away, but My words will not pass away.

34   "Be on guard, that your hearts may not be weighted down with dissipation and drunkenness and the worries of life, and that day come on you suddenly like a trap;

35   for it will come upon all those who dwell on the face of all the earth.

So, in answering the question "Why now?", we have shown from the reordered Revelation and the Gospels that the timing of the first seal being broken is near the time of the end of WW II. The evidence is the rise of the U.S. as a global power, the demise of totalitarianism in favor of democracy (the U.S. political and economic system) and the establishment of Israel. All of this happens at the same time that the U.S. begins its ride to bring freedom and democracy to the world. As the generation that saw the beginning of these events are in their 50s, terrorism takes peace from the world as prophesied in Seal 2 when the Red Horse rides. Then, within a short period of time, the global economy threatens collapse. The beast will not rise to power until Seal 5, but all of the end-time prophecies up to the return of Christ will all happen during the lifespan of this one generation.

This brings me to the world today as the last point to establish my case for us being in the end-times.

Are We the End-Time Generation: The World Today

Open a newspaper, turn on TV, scan a magazine or book stand, look at the popular songs, all will tell you that Satan is becoming bolder and growing in strength here on earth. This is the first time in recorded history when the word "bad" means "good" both literally and figuratively. Think of Michael Jackson's hit song. There has always been evil in the world and people have always done horrible things to each other, but this is the first time in history when society as a whole permits and in fact condones evil. What is the reaction to the rise of lawlessness and moral decay we see around us?

Matthew 24:12 "And because lawlessness is increased, most people's love will grow cold."

2 Tim 3:1-9

1   But realize this, that in the last days difficult times will come.

2   For men will be lovers of self, lovers of money, boastful, arrogant, revilers, disobedient to parents, ungrateful, unholy,

3   unloving, irreconcilable, malicious gossips, without self-control, brutal, haters of good,

4   treacherous, reckless, conceited, lovers of pleasure rather than lovers of God;

5   holding to a form of godliness, although they have denied its power; and avoid such men as these.

6   For among them are those who enter into households and captivate weak women weighed down with sins, led on by various impulses,

7   always learning and never able to come to the knowledge of the truth.

8   And just as Jannes and Jambres opposed Moses, so these {men} also oppose the truth, men of depraved mind, rejected as regards the faith.

9   But they will not make further progress; for their folly will be obvious to all, as also that of those {two} came to be.

2 Pet 3:3-4

3   Know this first of all, that in the last days mockers will come with {their} mocking, following after their own lusts,

4   and saying, "Where is the promise of His coming? For {ever} since the fathers fell asleep, all continues just as it was from the beginning of creation."

Jude 1:17-23

17   But you, beloved, ought to remember the words that were spoken beforehand by the apostles of our Lord Jesus Christ,

18   that they were saying to you, "In the last time there shall be mockers, following after their own ungodly lusts."

19   These are the ones who cause divisions, worldly-minded, devoid of the Spirit.

20   But you, beloved, building yourselves up on your most holy faith; praying in the Holy Spirit;

21   keep yourselves in the love of God, waiting anxiously for the mercy of our Lord Jesus Christ to eternal life.

22   And have mercy on some, who are doubting;

23   save others, snatching them out of the fire; and on some have mercy with fear, hating even the garment polluted by the flesh.

In other words people of the earth will become so self-centered they will not be concerned with the plight of others. We are beginning to see this today. Have you driven a car lately? Where is the courtesy we used to see? Where are our manners and civility? We are at the early stages, so many non-believers in God will still contribute to help the victims of major disasters and social causes, but many peoples hearts are hardening.

One of the main points of my discussion of Revelation is that the White Horse is bringing freedom, democracy, and a market based economy to the world. It is consistent that Satan will work to corrupt the good gifts that God gives to the world. He has corrupted freedom of speech into freedom to spread obscenities and pornography, freedom of religion into banning any reference of God in public places, freedom to bear arms into cop killing guns and ammunition, and freedom of assembly into permitting hate groups. Ethical standards now need to be taught in college and in the business world, because people don't know what ethical is.

What does the media say about Christians today? When you hear the term Christian in the press do you see us characterized as compassionate, moral leaders for our country and community or has the media labeled us as extremist political interest groups pushing a point of view.

We have labeled abortion as choice and now we are seeing scientists experimenting with genetically altering animals and eventually humans. If God does not begin the end-times, it would not be too many generations from now when families would need to have genetically engineered children to compete in the world economy. You have seen what science fiction has to say. All of this will be possible if things continue as they are.

Could it be clearer that we are nearing a time like the time of Babel in Genesis when God needed to interrupt the affairs of men? Interesting that Babel is a derivative of Babylon, which is the symbol of the great city of the beast in Revelation. I believe that God has timed the end-times to interrupt man's efforts to become god.

Finally, lets read again the prophecy of the Red Horse.

> Rev 6:4   And another, a <u>red horse</u>, went out; and to him who sat on it, it was granted to take peace from the earth, and that {men} should slay one another; and a great sword was given to him.

Isn't this exactly what is happening today? The U.S. and the rest of the world are engaged in a war on terrorism. It is as though Revelation was describing the scene. Extremists who do not represent a country are calling for death to those around the world who don't turn to their form of Islam and believe as they do. This is even happening to people of other Islamic faiths. Beheadings of innocent people, suicide bombings, U.S. military actions in Iraq and Afghanistan, and bombings in Europe and

Asia are the most obvious examples of the rise of the Red Horse. At the same time, wild fluctuations of economic markets, and oil prices over $100 a barrel are also signaling the beginning of events of Seal 3. This has become more obvious since I first published this book in 2007. Governments are working to prop up their banking systems from collapse. Thousands of undercover security actions are also taking place while the world invests to protect national and local communities. Communities will need to protect themselves from each other as Seal 4 is broken. The world is acting like Revelation says it will. What does all of this tell us?

The end-times have begun. I rest my case.

We Are the End-Time Generation: What Should You Do?

So what should you do in response to our being in the end-times? I believe the answer is to be alert so that you are not deceived, and to persevere. When you see the things happening that are discussed in Revelation, know that the end is near. The spirit will guide you to testify and offer yourself up for your beliefs as Jesus did, or allow you to escape death, witness what the earth will become, and join Christ in the air. Either way you will shortly be rewarded by God and spend the millennium and all eternity with Him. The second death will not touch you. You will be wed to Christ and be part of his family. And you will play an important role in Christ's kingdom as a son of God for all eternity.

Epilogue

I began this book by telling you that it was a devotional journey that transformed me. It was indeed. I want to share with you some of the ways it transformed me and challenge you.

1. I am in awe of the way that Revelation and other verses throughout the Bible come together to tell the story of the end-times. Using the Bible to interpret itself opened my eyes to things I would have never seen if I had used contemporary concepts as the basis for my journey. It shows the divine inspiration that touched Old and New Testament prophets, apostles, and authors of the sacred text. This further convinces me that the Bible contains the words God wants us to read as I describe in Key 2.

2. I now feel that I understand Revelation and many other parts of the Bible that I did not understand before. Before I would read the Bible like I would another book. Now I now pay close attention to the words used and relate them to what I have read elsewhere in the Bible. As I come across parts of scripture that I don't understand, I now have the faith that it is my understanding not the Bible that is lacking. That challenges me to dig deeper and pray harder for the Holy Spirit's help to find the answers that may be unique for me.

   This was exactly what happened as I was working to decide what wording I should put on the back cover of this book. I thought I should quote Jesus' words concerning the purpose of the revelation. God gave Jesus this revelation to show His bond- servants "the things which must <u>shortly</u> take place...". As I pulled this phrase out of the larger text I focused on the word shortly. Shortly...I wonder why he said shortly when it has been almost 2000 years. Then it hit me. I had always believed that this meant that in God's time scale a day is as a thousand years. But perhaps that isn't the right interpretation. The text says that the revelation is to show His bond-servants, but it does not say which ones. I had assumed it means all of them throughout history. I now believe another interpretation, that Revelation is addressed to the bond-servants who are living as we approach the end-times. Shortly is referring to the generation that would see the end of it all. If this is true, then it is only when that generation is alive that the revelation will be understood. Now is the time.

3. I now understand where heaven is and the details of the two resurrections that are described in the Bible. This has been particularly comforting for me, because while I was writing a new draft of this book my close friend, Greg Dwyer, died of cancer. He was with us for Christmas Eve and within six weeks he was with the Lord. I can now picture the scene that he is seeing in heaven from the descriptions in Revelation and know that the Lord will be giving him his white robe as he joins his family there.

4. I learned the importance of perseverance. This changed my entire view of adversity in my life. Tribulations are a way the Lord educates and refines us. Greg knew of perseverance. I spoke to him privately a week before he died. He was a good God-fearing man. I said to him that I certainly couldn't see God's plan in his illness and all the difficult times that he had faced....He said that it was hard for him to see also, but that he knew that his job was to make the best of the situation dealt him... and to be grateful for what he had, and God's job is to do what is in his plan......What a statement of faith and perseverance.

5. I have learned to view world events differently. The parallels between the news reports of Islamic extremists beheading people because they do not believe as they do are too close a parallel to the words in Revelation to be ignored. I believe that Christian believers around the world sense this. Now they can understand what is happening through the book of Revelation.

6. I now have the joy of knowing that eternity with the Lord is to be His priest and part of his government. It will not be an eternity of rest, but an eternity of active involvement with Him. As a person who spent most of my professional life working in government, I know the joy of serving and doing things that will improve people's lives. At FAA, I created the regulations that changed airline simulator training. This rule prevented aircraft accidents and provided better training for airline pilots. I always looked at this as a major accomplishment of my career. This is nothing compared to what it will be like to be part of Jesus Christ's kingdom.

7. Having written this book and given it to a number of people to read, I have discovered that the concepts in the book get people digging into their Bibles to see for themselves. Watching people challenge their prior views and engage with this book and the Bible is very exciting for me. It was from this insight that I came to feel that "Jesus Reveals Revelation" would be a great study guide for church adult bible study groups. It raises questions on many levels:
    a. What does the reordered scripture tell us that was hidden before?
    b. How does this interpretation compare to what we have read or been taught elsewhere?
    c. What do we conclude by discussing each Act of the Revelation?

    d. How can the Keys to Revelation help us understand other parts of the Bible?
    e. What do I need to do to prepare for what is ahead?
    f. How will this affect my life and my family?

The bottom line for me; writing this book has brought me closer to Jesus and given me the faith to face the future. While I know that difficult times are coming, I know what I need to do, and know with certainty that by persevering I will spend the millennium and eternity with Jesus. Seeing His words throughout the Bible open the doors of understanding to the book of Revelation has made me eager to listen to His Spirit as events unfold in my daily life.

I have taken you along on my devotional journey through Revelation. My journey actually began with my grandmother. Whenever I was about to go home after visiting her she would not say good-by. She would say, "read you Bible". And when I was old enough to do so, I did, almost every night. I challenge you to read your Bible and to continue your journey. Use the keys that I presented in Chapter 1 to continue your own spiritual journey through Revelation and the rest of the Bible. You might even read my book, "The Word & The Spirit: *How God Speaks to You*," to gain greater insight into the work of the Holy Spirit and God's desire to have a personal relationship with you. Your journey should include engaging with your family, neighbors, and people in your church to help each other as events in your life and the world progress. No matter what, keep your faith in God. Persevere at all cost. Read the Bible and let the Holy Spirit speak to you. Let love be your guiding principal. He is with you.

God bless you.

Appendix A: Definitions from the Bible

Term	Definition from the Bible	Reference
Abomination	Blood of the Saints	Rev 17:6
Alpha & Omega	God	Rev 1:8
Beast (First)	Anti-Christ/Satan in human form	Rev 13:4
Beast (Second)	False-Prophet	Rev 13:11
Bond-servants	Prophets, Saints, Those who fear God's name	Rev 11:18
Dragon	Serpent of old called the Devil and Satan	Rev 12:9
Eyes	Spirits of God sent into the earth (surveillance)	Rev 5:6
Heads	Kingdoms that have ruled the earth over time	Rev 17:10
Horns	Rulers that rise up in the end-times	Rev 17:12
Incense	Prayers of the saints	Rev 5:8
Lamb	Christ	Rev 5:8
Lamps	Spirits of God	Rev 4:5
Lamp stands	Churches	Rev 1:20
Olive Tree	God's chosen people	Rom11.19
Perseverance	Keeping God's word through adversity	Rev 3:10
Son of man	Christ	Rev 1: 13
Stars	Angels	Rev 1:20
Synagogues	Jews	Rev 3:9
Waters	Peoples, multitudes, nations, and tongues	Rev 17:15
Woman	Great City that rules over the kings of earth	Rev 17:18
Woe	One of last thee trumpets	Rev 8:13

Definitions from Context

Abomination of Desolation - Killer of the prophets,
	saints and believers	Rev 17:6
Elders	Patriarchs and Apostles	
Tribulation	An ordeal that causes difficulty, affliction, or death	
White	Pure / God's	Rev 6:2,
Witnesses	Moses and Paul	Rev 11:4

Definitional Hypothesis

Babylon	Symbol for the 7 great cities that reign over the global economic system through history.	Rev 17:18
Harlot	Political and economic system of the great cities.	Rev 17:3

Appendix B: Revelation Reordered

Below is the reordered Revelation in its entirety so that you can see the entire reordered book without my comment. I have retained the original references so that you can see where the text comes from. I have included this appendix so that you can read and see how the Spirit speaks to you as you read the reordered text without my comment or interaction. I have reordered Revelation into the following chapter order: 1, 2, 3, 12, 4, 5, 6a, 13, 17, 11a, 6b, 7, 8, 9a, 18, 9b, 14, 10, 11b, 15, 16, 19, 20, 21, 22.

Rev 1:1-20
CHAPTER 1

1   The Revelation of Jesus Christ, which God gave Him to show to His bond-servants, the things which must shortly take place; and He sent and communicated {it} by His angel to His bond-servant John,
2   who bore witness to the word of God and to the testimony of Jesus Christ, {even} to all that he saw.
3   Blessed is he who reads and those who hear the words of the prophecy, and heed the things which are written in it; for the time is near.
4   John to the seven churches that are in Asia: Grace to you and peace, from Him who is and who was and who is to come; and from the seven Spirits who are before His throne;
5   and from Jesus Christ, the faithful witness, the first-born of the dead, and the ruler of the kings of the earth. To Him who loves us, and released us from our sins by His blood,
6   and He has made us {to be} a kingdom, priests to His God and Father; to Him {be} the glory and the dominion forever and ever. Amen.

7	Behold, He is coming with the clouds, and every eye will see Him, even those who pierced Him; and all the tribes of the earth will mourn over Him. Even so. Amen.

8	"I am the Alpha and the Omega," says the Lord God, "who is and who was and who is to come, the Almighty."

9	I, John, your brother and fellow partaker in the tribulation and kingdom and perseverance {which are} in Jesus, was on the island called Patmos, because of the word of God and the testimony of Jesus.

10	I was in the Spirit on the Lord's day, and I heard behind me a loud voice like {the sound} of a trumpet,

11	saying, "Write in a book what you see, and send {it} to the seven churches: to Ephesus and to Smyrna and to Pergamum and to Thyatira and to Sardis and to Philadelphia and to Laodicea."

12	And I turned to see the voice that was speaking with me. And having turned I saw seven golden lampstands;

13	and in the middle of the lampstands one like a son of man, clothed in a robe reaching to the feet, and girded across His breast with a golden girdle.

14	And His head and His hair were white like white wool, like snow; and His eyes were like a flame of fire;

15	and His feet {were} like burnished bronze, when it has been caused to glow in a furnace, and His voice {was} like the sound of many waters.

16	And in His right hand He held seven stars; and out of His mouth came a sharp two-edged sword; and His face was like the sun shining in its strength.

17	And when I saw Him, I fell at His feet as a dead man. And He laid His right hand upon me, saying, "Do not be afraid; I am the first and the last,

18	and the living One; and I was dead, and behold, I am alive forevermore, and I have the keys of death and of Hades.

19	"Write therefore the things which you have seen, and the things which are, and the things which shall take place after these things.

20   "As for the mystery of the seven stars which you saw in My right hand, and the seven golden lampstands: the seven stars are the angels of the seven churches, and the seven lampstands are the seven churches.

Rev 2:1-29
CHAPTER 2

1   "To the angel of the church in Ephesus write: the One who holds the seven stars in His right hand, the One who walks among the seven golden lampstands, says this:
2   'I know your deeds and your toil and perseverance, and that you cannot endure evil men, and you put to the test those who call themselves apostles, and they are not, and you found them {to be} false;
3   and you have perseverance and have endured for My name's sake, and have not grown weary.
4   'But I have {this} against you, that you have left your first love.
5   'Remember therefore from where you have fallen, and repent and do the deeds you did at first; or else I am coming to you, and will remove your lampstand out of its place-- unless you repent.
6   'Yet this you do have, that you hate the deeds of the Nicolaitans, which I also hate.
7   'He who has an ear, let him hear what the Spirit says to the churches. To him who overcomes, I will grant to eat of the tree of life, which is in the Paradise of God.'
8   "And to the angel of the church in Smyrna write: The first and the last, who was dead, and has come to life, says this:
9   'I know your tribulation and your poverty (but you are rich), and the blasphemy by those who say they are Jews and are not, but are a synagogue of Satan.
10   'Do not fear what you are about to suffer. Behold, the devil is about to cast some of you into prison, that you may be tested,

and you will have tribulation ten days. Be faithful until death, and I will give you the crown of life.

11   'He who has an ear, let him hear what the Spirit says to the churches. He who overcomes shall not be hurt by the second death.'

12   "And to the angel of the church in Pergamum write: The One who has the sharp two-edged sword says this:

13   'I know where you dwell, where Satan's throne is; and you hold fast My name, and did not deny My faith, even in the days of Antipas, My witness, My faithful one, who was killed among you, where Satan dwells.

14   'But I have a few things against you, because you have there some who hold the teaching of Balaam, who kept teaching Balak to put a stumbling block before the sons of Israel, to eat things sacrificed to idols, and to commit {acts of} immorality.

15   'Thus you also have some who in the same way hold the teaching of the Nicolaitans.

16   'Repent therefore; or else I am coming to you quickly, and I will make war against them with the sword of My mouth.

17   'He who has an ear, let him hear what the Spirit says to the churches. To him who overcomes, to him I will give {some} of the hidden manna, and I will give him a white stone, and a new name written on the stone which no one knows but he who receives it.'

18   "And to the angel of the church in Thyatira write: The Son of God, who has eyes like a flame of fire, and His feet are like burnished bronze, says this:

19   'I know your deeds, and your love and faith and service and perseverance, and that your deeds of late are greater than at first.

20   'But I have {this} against you, that you tolerate the woman Jezebel, who calls herself a prophetess, and she teaches and leads My bond-servants astray, so that they commit {acts of} immorality and eat things sacrificed to idols.

21   'And I gave her time to repent; and she does not want to repent of her immorality.

22   'Behold, I will cast her upon a bed {of sickness} and those who commit adultery with her into great tribulation, unless they repent of her deeds.

23   'And I will kill her children with pestilence; and all the churches will know that I am He who searches the minds and hearts; and I will give to each one of you according to your deeds.

24   'But I say to you, the rest who are in Thyatira, who do not hold this teaching, who have not known the deep things of Satan, as they call them-- I place no other burden on you.

25   'Nevertheless what you have, hold fast until I come.

26   'And he who overcomes, and he who keeps My deeds until the end, to him I will give authority over the nations;

27   and he shall rule them with a rod of iron, as the vessels of the potter are broken to pieces, as I also have received {authority} from My Father;

28   and I will give him the morning star.

29   'He who has an ear, let him hear what the Spirit says to the churches.'

Rev 3:1-22
CHAPTER 3

1   "And to the angel of the church in Sardis write: He who has the seven Spirits of God, and the seven stars, says this: 'I know your deeds, that you have a name that you are alive, but you are dead.

2   'Wake up, and strengthen the things that remain, which were about to die; for I have not found your deeds completed in the sight of My God.

3   'Remember therefore what you have received and heard; and keep {it,} and repent. If therefore you will not wake up, I will come like a thief, and you will not know at what hour I will come upon you.

4   'But you have a few people in Sardis who have not soiled their garments; and they will walk with Me in white; for they are worthy.

5   'He who overcomes shall thus be clothed in white garments; and I will not erase his name from the book of life, and I will confess his name before My Father, and before His angels.

6   'He who has an ear, let him hear what the Spirit says to the churches.'

7   "And to the angel of the church in Philadelphia write: He who is holy, who is true, who has the key of David, who opens and no one will shut, and who shuts and no one opens, says this:

8   'I know your deeds. Behold, I have put before you an open door which no one can shut, because you have a little power, and have kept My word, and have not denied My name.

9   'Behold, I will cause {those} of the synagogue of Satan, who say that they are Jews, and are not, but lie-- behold, I will make them to come and bow down at your feet, and to know that I have loved you.

10   'Because you have kept the word of My perseverance, I also will keep you from the hour of testing, that {hour} which is about to come upon the whole world, to test those who dwell upon the earth.

11   'I am coming quickly; hold fast what you have, in order that no one take your crown.

12   'He who overcomes, I will make him a pillar in the temple of My God, and he will not go out from it anymore; and I will write upon him the name of My God, and the name of the city of My God, the new Jerusalem, which comes down out of heaven from My God, and My new name.

13   'He who has an ear, let him hear what the Spirit says to the churches.'

14   "And to the angel of the church in Laodicea write: The Amen, the faithful and true Witness, the Beginning of the creation of God, says this:

15   'I know your deeds, that you are neither cold nor hot; I would that you were cold or hot.

16   'So because you are lukewarm, and neither hot nor cold, I will spit you out of My mouth.

17   'Because you say, "I am rich, and have become wealthy, and have need of nothing," and you do not know that you are wretched and miserable and poor and blind and naked,

18   I advise you to buy from Me gold refined by fire, that you may become rich, and white garments, that you may clothe yourself, and {that} the shame of your nakedness may not be revealed; and eye salve to anoint your eyes, that you may see.

19   'Those whom I love, I reprove and discipline; be zealous therefore, and repent.

20   'Behold, I stand at the door and knock; if anyone hears My voice and opens the door, I will come in to him, and will dine with him, and he with Me.

21   'He who overcomes, I will grant to him to sit down with Me on My throne, as I also overcame and sat down with My Father on His throne.

22   'He who has an ear, let him hear what the Spirit says to the churches.' "

Rev 12:1-17
CHAPTER 12

1   And a great sign appeared in heaven: a woman clothed with the sun, and the moon under her feet, and on her head a crown of twelve stars;

2   and she was with child; and she cried out, being in labor and in pain to give birth.

3   And another sign appeared in heaven: and behold, a great red dragon having seven heads and ten horns, and on his heads {were} seven diadems.

4   And his tail swept away a third of the stars of heaven, and threw them to the earth. And the dragon stood before the woman

who was about to give birth, so that when she gave birth he might devour her child.

5   And she gave birth to a son, a male {child} who is to rule all the nations with a rod of iron; and her child was caught up to God and to His throne.

6   And the woman fled into the wilderness where she had a place prepared by God, so that there she might be nourished for one thousand two hundred and sixty days.

7   And there was war in heaven, Michael and his angels waging war with the dragon. And the dragon and his angels waged war,

8   and they were not strong enough, and there was no longer a place found for them in heaven.

9   And the great dragon was thrown down, the serpent of old who is called the devil and Satan, who deceives the whole world; he was thrown down to the earth, and his angels were thrown down with him.

10   And I heard a loud voice in heaven, saying, "Now the salvation, and the power, and the kingdom of our God and the authority of His Christ have come, for the accuser of our brethren has been thrown down, who accuses them before our God day and night.

11   "And they overcame him because of the blood of the Lamb and because of the word of their testimony, and they did not love their life even to death.

12   "For this reason, rejoice, O heavens and you who dwell in them. Woe to the earth and the sea, because the devil has come down to you, having great wrath, knowing that he has {only} a short time."

13   And when the dragon saw that he was thrown down to the earth, he persecuted the woman who gave birth to the male {child.}

14   And the two wings of the great eagle were given to the woman, in order that she might fly into the wilderness to her place, where she was nourished for a time and times and half a time, from the presence of the serpent.

15   And the serpent poured water like a river out of his mouth after the woman, so that he might cause her to be swept away with the flood.
16   And the earth helped the woman, and the earth opened its mouth and drank up the river which the dragon poured out of his mouth.
17   And the dragon was enraged with the woman, and went off to make war with the rest of her offspring, who keep the commandments of God and hold to the testimony of Jesus.

Rev 4:1-11
CHAPTER 4

1   After these things I looked, and behold, a door {standing} open in heaven, and the first voice which I had heard, like {the sound} of a trumpet speaking with me, said, "Come up here, and I will show you what must take place after these things."
2   Immediately I was in the Spirit; and behold, a throne was standing in heaven, and One sitting on the throne.
3   And He who was sitting {was} like a jasper stone and a sardius in appearance; and {there was} a rainbow around the throne, like an emerald in appearance.
4   And around the throne {were} twenty-four thrones; and upon the thrones {I saw} twenty-four elders sitting, clothed in white garments, and golden crowns on their heads.
5   And from the throne proceed flashes of lightning and sounds and peals of thunder. And {there were} seven lamps of fire burning before the throne, which are the seven Spirits of God;
6   and before the throne {there was,} as it were, a sea of glass like crystal; and in the center and around the throne, four living creatures full of eyes in front and behind.
7   And the first creature {was} like a lion, and the second creature like a calf, and the third creature had a face like that of a man, and the fourth creature {was} like a flying eagle.

8　　And the four living creatures, each one of them having six wings, are full of eyes around and within; and day and night they do not cease to say, "Holy, holy, holy, {is} the Lord God, the Almighty, who was and who is and who is to come."

9　　And when the living creatures give glory and honor and thanks to Him who sits on the throne, to Him who lives forever and ever,

10　　the twenty-four elders will fall down before Him who sits on the throne, and will worship Him who lives forever and ever, and will cast their crowns before the throne, saying,

11　　"Worthy art Thou, our Lord and our God, to receive glory and honor and power; for Thou didst create all things, and because of Thy will they existed, and were created."

Rev 5:1-14
CHAPTER 5

1　　And I saw in the right hand of Him who sat on the throne a book written inside and on the back, sealed up with seven seals.

2　　And I saw a strong angel proclaiming with a loud voice, "Who is worthy to open the book and to break its seals?"

3　　And no one in heaven, or on the earth, or under the earth, was able to open the book, or to look into it.

4　　And I {began} to weep greatly, because no one was found worthy to open the book, or to look into it;

5　　and one of the elders said to me, "Stop weeping; behold, the Lion that is from the tribe of Judah, the Root of David, has overcome so as to open the book and its seven seals."

6　　And I saw between the throne (with the four living creatures) and the elders a Lamb standing, as if slain, having seven horns and seven eyes, which are the seven Spirits of God, sent out into all the earth.

7　　And He came, and He took {it} out of the right hand of Him who sat on the throne.

8　　And when He had taken the book, the four living creatures and the twenty-four elders fell down before the Lamb, having each one a harp, and golden bowls full of incense, which are the prayers of the saints.

9   And they sang a new song, saying, "Worthy art Thou to take the book, and to break its seals; for Thou wast slain, and didst purchase for God with Thy blood {men} from every tribe and tongue and people and nation.

10   "And Thou hast made them {to be} a kingdom and priests to our God; and they will reign upon the earth."

11   And I looked, and I heard the voice of many angels around the throne and the living creatures and the elders; and the number of them was myriads of myriads, and thousands of thousands,

12   saying with a loud voice, "Worthy is the Lamb that was slain to receive power and riches and wisdom and might and honor and glory and blessing."

13   And every created thing which is in heaven and on the earth and under the earth and on the sea, and all things in them, I heard saying, "To Him who sits on the throne, and to the Lamb, {be} blessing and honor and glory and dominion forever and ever."

14   And the four living creatures kept saying, "Amen." And the elders fell down and worshiped.

Rev 6:1-11
CHAPTER 6

1   And I saw when the Lamb broke one of the seven seals, and I heard one of the four living creatures saying as with a voice of thunder, "Come."

2   And I looked, and behold, a white horse, and he who sat on it had a bow; and a crown was given to him; and he went out conquering, and to conquer.

3   And when He broke the second seal, I heard the second living creature saying, "Come."

4   And another, a red horse, went out; and to him who sat on it, it was granted to take peace from the earth, and that {men} should slay one another; and a great sword was given to him.

5   And when He broke the third seal, I heard the third living creature saying, "Come." And I looked, and behold, a black horse; and he who sat on it had a pair of scales in his hand.

6   And I heard as it were a voice in the center of the four living creatures saying, "A quart of wheat for a denarius, and three quarts of barley for a denarius; and do not harm the oil and the wine."

7   And when He broke the fourth seal, I heard the voice of the fourth living creature saying, "Come."

8   And I looked, and behold, an ashen horse; and he who sat on it had the name Death; and Hades was following with him. And authority was given to them over a fourth of the earth, to kill with sword and with famine and with pestilence and by the wild beasts of the earth.

9   And when He broke the fifth seal, I saw underneath the altar the souls of those who had been slain because of the word of God, and because of the testimony which they had maintained;

10   and they cried out with a loud voice, saying, "How long, O Lord, holy and true, wilt Thou refrain from judging and avenging our blood on those who dwell on the earth?"

11   And there was given to each of them a white robe; and they were told that they should rest for a little while longer, until {the number of} their fellow servants and their brethren who were to be killed even as they had been, should be completed also.

Rev 13:1-18
CHAPTER 13

1   And he stood on the sand of the seashore. And I saw a beast coming up out of the sea, having ten horns and seven heads, and on his horns {were} ten diadems, and on his heads {were} blasphemous names.

2   And the beast which I saw was like a leopard, and his feet were like {those} of a bear, and his mouth like the mouth of a lion. And the dragon gave him his power and his throne and great authority.

3   And {I saw} one of his heads as if it had been slain, and his fatal wound was healed. And the whole earth was amazed {and followed} after the beast;

4   and they worshiped the dragon, because he gave his authority to the beast; and they worshiped the beast, saying, "Who is like the beast, and who is able to wage war with him?"

5   And there was given to him a mouth speaking arrogant words and blasphemies; and authority to act for forty-two months was given to him.

6   And he opened his mouth in blasphemies against God, to blaspheme His name and His tabernacle, {that is} those who dwell in heaven.

7   And it was given to him to make war with the saints and to overcome them; and authority over every tribe and people and tongue and nation was given to him.

8   And all who dwell on the earth will worship him, {everyone} whose name has not been written from the foundation of the world in the book of life of the Lamb who has been slain.

9   If anyone has an ear, let him hear.

10   If anyone {is destined} for captivity, to captivity he goes; if anyone kills with the sword, with the sword he must be killed. Here is the perseverance and the faith of the saints.

11   And I saw another beast coming up out of the earth; and he had two horns like a lamb, and he spoke as a dragon.

12   And he exercises all the authority of the first beast in his presence. And he makes the earth and those who dwell in it to worship the first beast, whose fatal wound was healed.

13   And he performs great signs, so that he even makes fire come down out of heaven to the earth in the presence of men.

14   And he deceives those who dwell on the earth because of the signs which it was given him to perform in the presence of

the beast, telling those who dwell on the earth to make an image to the beast who had the wound of the sword and has come to life.

15   And there was given to him to give breath to the image of the beast, that the image of the beast might even speak and cause as many as do not worship the image of the beast to be killed.

16   And he causes all, the small and the great, and the rich and the poor, and the free men and the slaves, to be given a mark on their right hand, or on their forehead,

17   and {he provides} that no one should be able to buy or to sell, except the one who has the mark, {either} the name of the beast or the number of his name.

18   Here is wisdom. Let him who has understanding calculate the number of the beast, for the number is that of a man; and his number is six hundred and sixty-six.

Rev 17:1-18
CHAPTER 17

1   And one of the seven angels who had the seven bowls came and spoke with me, saying, "Come here, I shall show you the judgment of the great harlot who sits on many waters,

2   with whom the kings of the earth committed {acts of} immorality, and those who dwell on the earth were made drunk with the wine of her immorality."

3   And he carried me away in the Spirit into a wilderness; and I saw a woman sitting on a scarlet beast, full of blasphemous names, having seven heads and ten horns.

4   And the woman was clothed in purple and scarlet, and adorned with gold and precious stones and pearls, having in her hand a gold cup full of abominations and of the unclean things of her immorality,

5   and upon her forehead a name {was} written, a mystery, "BABYLON THE GREAT, THE MOTHER OF HARLOTS AND OF THE ABOMINATIONS OF THE EARTH."

6   And I saw the woman drunk with the blood of the saints, and with the blood of the witnesses of Jesus. And when I saw her, I wondered greatly.

7   And the angel said to me, "Why do you wonder? I shall tell you the mystery of the woman and of the beast that carries her, which has the seven heads and the ten horns.

8   "The beast that you saw was and is not, and is about to come up out of the abyss and to go to destruction. And those who dwell on the earth will wonder, whose name has not been written in the book of life from the foundation of the world, when they see the beast, that he was and is not and will come.

9   "Here is the mind which has wisdom. The seven heads are seven mountains on which the woman sits,

10   and they are seven kings; five have fallen, one is, the other has not yet come; and when he comes, he must remain a little while.

11   "And the beast which was and is not, is himself also an eighth, and is {one} of the seven, and he goes to destruction.

12   "And the ten horns which you saw are ten kings, who have not yet received a kingdom, but they receive authority as kings with the beast for one hour.

13   "These have one purpose and they give their power and authority to the beast.

14   "These will wage war against the Lamb, and the Lamb will overcome them, because He is Lord of lords and King of kings, and those who are with Him {are the} called and chosen and faithful."

15   And he said to me, "The waters which you saw where the harlot sits, are peoples and multitudes and nations and tongues.

16   "And the ten horns which you saw, and the beast, these will hate the harlot and will make her desolate and naked, and will eat her flesh and will burn her up with fire.

17   "For God has put it in their hearts to execute His purpose by having a common purpose, and by giving their kingdom to the beast, until the words of God should be fulfilled.

18   "And the woman whom you saw is the great city, which reigns over the kings of the earth."

Rev 11:1-13
CHAPTER 11

1   And there was given me a measuring rod like a staff; and someone said, "Rise and measure the temple of God, and the altar, and those who worship in it.
2   "And leave out the court which is outside the temple, and do not measure it, for it has been given to the nations; and they will tread under foot the holy city for forty-two months.
3   "And I will grant {authority} to my two witnesses, and they will prophesy for twelve hundred and sixty days, clothed in sackcloth."
4   These are the two olive trees and the two lampstands that stand before the Lord of the earth.
5   And if anyone desires to harm them, fire proceeds out of their mouth and devours their enemies; and if anyone would desire to harm them, in this manner he must be killed.
6   These have the power to shut up the sky, in order that rain may not fall during the days of their prophesying; and they have power over the waters to turn them into blood, and to smite the earth with every plague, as often as they desire.
7   And when they have finished their testimony, the beast that comes up out of the abyss will make war with them, and overcome them and kill them.
8   And their dead bodies {will lie} in the street of the great city which mystically is called Sodom and Egypt, where also their Lord was crucified.
9   And those from the peoples and tribes and tongues and nations {will} look at their dead bodies for three and a half days, and will not permit their dead bodies to be laid in a tomb.
10   And those who dwell on the earth {will} rejoice over them and make merry; and they will send gifts to one another,

because these two prophets tormented those who dwell on the earth.

11   And after the three and a half days the breath of life from God came into them, and they stood on their feet; and great fear fell upon those who were beholding them.

12   And they heard a loud voice from heaven saying to them, "Come up here." And they went up into heaven in the cloud, and their enemies beheld them.

13   And in that hour there was a great earthquake, and a tenth of the city fell; and seven thousand people were killed in the earthquake, and the rest were terrified and gave glory to the God of heaven.

Rev 6:12-17

12   And I looked when He broke the sixth seal, and there was a great earthquake; and the sun became black as sackcloth {made} of hair, and the whole moon became like blood;

13   and the stars of the sky fell to the earth, as a fig tree casts its unripe figs when shaken by a great wind.

14   And the sky was split apart like a scroll when it is rolled up; and every mountain and island were moved out of their places.

15   And the kings of the earth and the great men and the commanders and the rich and the strong and every slave and free man, hid themselves in the caves and among the rocks of the mountains;

16   and they said to the mountains and to the rocks, "Fall on us and hide us from the presence of Him who sits on the throne, and from the wrath of the Lamb;

17   for the great day of their wrath has come; and who is able to stand?"

Rev 7:1-17
CHAPTER 7

1   After this I saw four angels standing at the four corners of the earth, holding back the four winds of the earth, so that no wind should blow on the earth or on the sea or on any tree.

2   And I saw another angel ascending from the rising of the sun, having the seal of the living God; and he cried out with a loud voice to the four angels to whom it was granted to harm the earth and the sea,

3   saying, "Do not harm the earth or the sea or the trees, until we have sealed the bond-servants of our God on their foreheads."

4   And I heard the number of those who were sealed, one hundred and forty-four thousand sealed from every tribe of the sons of Israel:

5   from the tribe of Judah, twelve thousand {were} sealed, from the tribe of Reuben twelve thousand, from the tribe of Gad twelve thousand,

6   from the tribe of Asher twelve thousand, from the tribe of Naphtali twelve thousand, from the tribe of Manasseh twelve thousand,

7   from the tribe of Simeon twelve thousand, from the tribe of Levi twelve thousand, from the tribe of Issachar twelve thousand,

8   from the tribe of Zebulun twelve thousand, from the tribe of Joseph twelve thousand, from the tribe of Benjamin, twelve thousand {were} sealed.

9   After these things I looked, and behold, a great multitude, which no one could count, from every nation and {all} tribes and peoples and tongues, standing before the throne and before the Lamb, clothed in white robes, and palm branches {were} in their hands;

10   and they cry out with a loud voice, saying, "Salvation to our God who sits on the throne, and to the Lamb."

11   And all the angels were standing around the throne and {around} the elders and the four living creatures; and they fell on their faces before the throne and worshiped God,

12   saying, "Amen, blessing and glory and wisdom and thanksgiving and honor and power and might, {be} to our God forever and ever. Amen."

13   And one of the elders answered, saying to me, "These who are clothed in the white robes, who are they, and from where have they come?"

14   And I said to him, "My lord, you know." And he said to me, "These are the ones who come out of the great tribulation, and they have washed their robes and made them white in the blood of the Lamb.

15   "For this reason, they are before the throne of God; and they serve Him day and night in His temple; and He who sits on the throne shall spread His tabernacle over them.

16   "They shall hunger no more, neither thirst anymore; neither shall the sun beat down on them, nor any heat;

17   for the Lamb in the center of the throne shall be their shepherd, and shall guide them to springs of the water of life; and God shall wipe every tear from their eyes."

Rev 8:1-13
CHAPTER 8

1   And when He broke the seventh seal, there was silence in heaven for about half an hour.

2   And I saw the seven angels who stand before God; and seven trumpets were given to them.

3   And another angel came and stood at the altar, holding a golden censer; and much incense was given to him, that he might add it to the prayers of all the saints upon the golden altar which was before the throne.

4   And the smoke of the incense, with the prayers of the saints, went up before God out of the angel's hand.

5   And the angel took the censer; and he filled it with the fire of the altar and threw it to the earth; and there followed peals of thunder and sounds and flashes of lightning and an earthquake.
6   And the seven angels who had the seven trumpets prepared themselves to sound them.
7   And the first sounded, and there came hail and fire, mixed with blood, and they were thrown to the earth; and a third of the earth was burned up, and a third of the trees were burned up, and all the green grass was burned up.
8   And the second angel sounded, and {something} like a great mountain burning with fire was thrown into the sea; and a third of the sea became blood;
9   and a third of the creatures, which were in the sea and had life, died; and a third of the ships were destroyed.
10   And the third angel sounded, and a great star fell from heaven, burning like a torch, and it fell on a third of the rivers and on the springs of waters;
11   and the name of the star is called Wormwood; and a third of the waters became wormwood; and many men died from the waters, because they were made bitter.
12   And the fourth angel sounded, and a third of the sun and a third of the moon and a third of the stars were smitten, so that a third of them might be darkened and the day might not shine for a third of it, and the night in the same way.
13   And I looked, and I heard an eagle flying in midheaven, saying with a loud voice, "Woe, woe, woe, to those who dwell on the earth, because of the remaining blasts of the trumpet of the three angels who are about to sound!"

Rev 9:1-12
CHAPTER 9

1   And the fifth angel sounded, and I saw a star from heaven which had fallen to the earth; and the key of the bottomless pit was given to him.

2   And he opened the bottomless pit; and smoke went up out of the pit, like the smoke of a great furnace; and the sun and the air were darkened by the smoke of the pit.

3   And out of the smoke came forth locusts upon the earth; and power was given them, as the scorpions of the earth have power.

4   And they were told that they should not hurt the grass of the earth, nor any green thing, nor any tree, but only the men who do not have the seal of God on their foreheads.

5   And they were not permitted to kill anyone, but to torment for five months; and their torment was like the torment of a scorpion when it stings a man.

6   And in those days men will seek death and will not find it; and they will long to die and death flees from them.

7   And the appearance of the locusts was like horses prepared for battle; and on their heads, as it were, crowns like gold, and their faces were like the faces of men.

8   And they had hair like the hair of women, and their teeth were like {the teeth} of lions.

9   And they had breastplates like breastplates of iron; and the sound of their wings was like the sound of chariots, of many horses rushing to battle.

10   And they have tails like scorpions, and stings; and in their tails is their power to hurt men for five months.

11   They have as king over them, the angel of the abyss; his name in Hebrew is Abaddon, and in the Greek he has the name Apollyon.

12   The first woe is past; behold, two woes are still coming after these things.

Rev 18:1-24
CHAPTER 18

1   After these things I saw another angel coming down from heaven, having great authority, and the earth was illumined with his glory.

2   And he cried out with a mighty voice, saying, "Fallen, fallen is Babylon the great! And she has become a dwelling place of demons and a prison of every unclean spirit, and a prison of every unclean and hateful bird.

3   "For all the nations have drunk of the wine of the passion of her immorality, and the kings of the earth have committed {acts of} immorality with her, and the merchants of the earth have become rich by the wealth of her sensuality."

4   And I heard another voice from heaven, saying, "Come out of her, my people, that you may not participate in her sins and that you may not receive of her plagues;

5   for her sins have piled up as high as heaven, and God has remembered her iniquities.

6   "Pay her back even as she has paid, and give back {to her} double according to her deeds; in the cup which she has mixed, mix twice as much for her.

7   "To the degree that she glorified herself and lived sensuously, to the same degree give her torment and mourning; for she says in her heart, 'I sit {as} a queen and I am not a widow, and will never see mourning.'

8   "For this reason in one day her plagues will come, pestilence and mourning and famine, and she will be burned up with fire; for the Lord God who judges her is strong.

9   "And the kings of the earth, who committed {acts of} immorality and lived sensuously with her, will weep and lament over her when they see the smoke of her burning,

10   standing at a distance because of the fear of her torment, saying, 'Woe, woe, the great city, Babylon, the strong city! For in one hour your judgment has come.'

11   "And the merchants of the earth weep and mourn over her, because no one buys their cargoes any more;

12   cargoes of gold and silver and precious stones and pearls and fine linen and purple and silk and scarlet, and every {kind of} citron wood and every article of ivory and every article {made} from very costly wood and bronze and iron and marble,

13   and cinnamon and spice and incense and perfume and frankincense and wine and olive oil and fine flour and wheat and cattle and sheep, and {cargoes} of horses and chariots and slaves and human lives.

14   "And the fruit you long for has gone from you, and all things that were luxurious and splendid have passed away from you and {men} will no longer find them.

15   "The merchants of these things, who became rich from her, will stand at a distance because of the fear of her torment, weeping and mourning,

16   saying, 'Woe, woe, the great city, she who was clothed in fine linen and purple and scarlet, and adorned with gold and precious stones and pearls;

17   for in one hour such great wealth has been laid waste!' And every shipmaster and every passenger and sailor, and as many as make their living by the sea, stood at a distance,

18   and were crying out as they saw the smoke of her burning, saying,' What {city} is like the great city? '

19   "And they threw dust on their heads and were crying out, weeping and mourning, saying, 'Woe, woe, the great city, in which all who had ships at sea became rich by her wealth, for in one hour she has been laid waste!'

20   "Rejoice over her, O heaven, and you saints and apostles and prophets, because God has pronounced judgment for you against her."

21   And a strong angel took up a stone like a great millstone and threw it into the sea, saying, "Thus will Babylon, the great city, be thrown down with violence, and will not be found any longer.

22   "And the sound of harpists and musicians and flute-players and trumpeters will not be heard in you any longer; and no craftsman of any craft will be found in you any longer; and the sound of a mill will not be heard in you any longer;

23   and the light of a lamp will not shine in you any longer; and the voice of the bridegroom and bride will not be heard in

you any longer; for your merchants were the great men of the earth, because all the nations were deceived by your sorcery.
24   "And in her was found the blood of prophets and of saints and of all who have been slain on the earth."

Rev 9:13-21
13   And the sixth angel sounded, and I heard a voice from the four horns of the golden altar which is before God,
14   one saying to the sixth angel who had the trumpet, "Release the four angels who are bound at the great river Euphrates."
15   And the four angels, who had been prepared for the hour and day and month and year, were released, so that they might kill a third of mankind.
16   And the number of the armies of the horsemen was two hundred million; I heard the number of them.
17   And this is how I saw in the vision the horses and those who sat on them: {the riders} had breastplates {the color} of fire and of hyacinth and of brimstone; and the heads of the horses are like the heads of lions; and out of their mouths proceed fire and smoke and brimstone.
18   A third of mankind was killed by these three plagues, by the fire and the smoke and the brimstone, which proceeded out of their mouths.
19   For the power of the horses is in their mouths and in their tails; for their tails are like serpents and have heads; and with them they do harm.
20   And the rest of mankind, who were not killed by these plagues, did not repent of the works of their hands, so as not to worship demons, and the idols of gold and of silver and of brass and of stone and of wood, which can neither see nor hear nor walk;
21   and they did not repent of their murders nor of their sorceries nor of their immorality nor of their thefts.
(NAS)

Rev 14:1-20
CHAPTER 14

1   And I looked, and behold, the Lamb {was} standing on Mount Zion, and with Him one hundred and forty-four thousand, having His name and the name of His Father written on their foreheads.

2   And I heard a voice from heaven, like the sound of many waters and like the sound of loud thunder, and the voice which I heard {was} like {the sound} of harpists playing on their harps.

3   And they sang a new song before the throne and before the four living creatures and the elders; and no one could learn the song except the one hundred and forty-four thousand who had been purchased from the earth.

4   These are the ones who have not been defiled with women, for they have kept themselves chaste. These {are} the ones who follow the Lamb wherever He goes. These have been purchased from among men as first fruits to God and to the Lamb.

5   And no lie was found in their mouth; they are blameless.

6   And I saw another angel flying in midheaven, having an eternal gospel to preach to those who live on the earth, and to every nation and tribe and tongue and people;

7   and he said with a loud voice, "Fear God, and give Him glory, because the hour of His judgment has come; and worship Him who made the heaven and the earth and sea and springs of waters."

8   And another angel, a second one, followed, saying, "Fallen, fallen is Babylon the great, she who has made all the nations drink of the wine of the passion of her immorality."

9   And another angel, a third one, followed them, saying with a loud voice, "If anyone worships the beast and his image, and receives a mark on his forehead or upon his hand,

10   he also will drink of the wine of the wrath of God, which is mixed in full strength in the cup of His anger; and he will be

tormented with fire and brimstone in the presence of the holy angels and in the presence of the Lamb.

11   "And the smoke of their torment goes up forever and ever; and they have no rest day and night, those who worship the beast and his image, and whoever receives the mark of his name."

12   Here is the perseverance of the saints who keep the commandments of God and their faith in Jesus.

13   And I heard a voice from heaven, saying, "Write, 'Blessed are the dead who die in the Lord from now on!'" "Yes," says the Spirit, "that they may rest from their labors, for their deeds follow with them."

14   And I looked, and behold, a white cloud, and sitting on the cloud {was} one like a son of man, having a golden crown on His head, and a sharp sickle in His hand.

15   And another angel came out of the temple, crying out with a loud voice to Him who sat on the cloud, "Put in your sickle and reap, because the hour to reap has come, because the harvest of the earth is ripe."

16   And He who sat on the cloud swung His sickle over the earth; and the earth was reaped.

17   And another angel came out of the temple which is in heaven, and he also had a sharp sickle.

18   And another angel, the one who has power over fire, came out from the altar; and he called with a loud voice to him who had the sharp sickle, saying, "Put in your sharp sickle, and gather the clusters from the vine of the earth, because her grapes are ripe."

19   And the angel swung his sickle to the earth, and gathered {the clusters from} the vine of the earth, and threw them into the great wine press of the wrath of God.

20   And the wine press was trodden outside the city, and blood came out from the wine press, up to the horses' bridles, for a distance of two hundred miles.

Rev 10:1-11
CHAPTER 10

1   And I saw another strong angel coming down out of heaven, clothed with a cloud; and the rainbow was upon his head, and his face was like the sun, and his feet like pillars of fire;
2   and he had in his hand a little book which was open. And he placed his right foot on the sea and his left on the land;
3   and he cried out with a loud voice, as when a lion roars; and when he had cried out, the seven peals of thunder uttered their voices.
4   And when the seven peals of thunder had spoken, I was about to write; and I heard a voice from heaven saying, "Seal up the things which the seven peals of thunder have spoken, and do not write them."
5   And the angel whom I saw standing on the sea and on the land lifted up his right hand to heaven,
6   and swore by Him who lives forever and ever, who created heaven and the things in it, and the earth and the things in it, and the sea and the things in it, that there shall be delay no longer,
7   but in the days of the voice of the seventh angel, when he is about to sound, then the mystery of God is finished, as He preached to His servants the prophets.
8   And the voice which I heard from heaven, {I heard} again speaking with me, and saying, "Go, take the book which is open in the hand of the angel who stands on the sea and on the land."
9   And I went to the angel, telling him to give me the little book. And he said to me, "Take it, and eat it; and it will make your stomach bitter, but in your mouth it will be sweet as honey."
10   And I took the little book out of the angel's hand and ate it, and it was in my mouth sweet as honey; and when I had eaten it, my stomach was made bitter.

11   And they said to me, "You must prophesy again concerning many peoples and nations and tongues and kings." (NAS)

Rev 11:14-19
CHAPTER 11

14 The second woe is past; behold, the third woe is coming quickly.
15   And the seventh angel sounded; and there arose loud voices in heaven, saying, "The kingdom of the world has become {the kingdom} of our Lord, and of His Christ; and He will reign forever and ever."
16   And the twenty-four elders, who sit on their thrones before God, fell on their faces and worshiped God,
17   saying, "We give Thee thanks, O Lord God, the Almighty, who art and who wast, because Thou hast taken Thy great power and hast begun to reign.
18   "And the nations were enraged, and Thy wrath came, and the time {came} for the dead to be judged, and {the time} to give their reward to Thy bond-servants the prophets and to the saints and to those who fear Thy name, the small and the great, and to destroy those who destroy the earth."
19   And the temple of God which is in heaven was opened; and the ark of His covenant appeared in His temple, and there were flashes of lightning and sounds and peals of thunder and an earthquake and a great hailstorm.

Rev 15:1-8
CHAPTER 15

1   And I saw another sign in heaven, great and marvelous, seven angels who had seven plagues, {which are} the last, because in them the wrath of God is finished.
2   And I saw, as it were, a sea of glass mixed with fire, and those who had come off victorious from the beast and from his

image and from the number of his name, standing on the sea of glass, holding harps of God.

3	And they sang the song of Moses the bond-servant of God and the song of the Lamb, saying, "Great and marvelous are Thy works, O Lord God, the Almighty; Righteous and true are Thy ways, Thou King of the nations.

4	"Who will not fear, O Lord, and glorify Thy name? For Thou alone art holy; for all the nations will come and worship before Thee, for Thy righteous acts have been revealed."

5	After these things I looked, and the temple of the tabernacle of testimony in heaven was opened,

6	and the seven angels who had the seven plagues came out of the temple, clothed in linen, clean {and} bright, and girded around their breasts with golden girdles.

7	And one of the four living creatures gave to the seven angels seven golden bowls full of the wrath of God, who lives forever and ever.

8	And the temple was filled with smoke from the glory of God and from His power; and no one was able to enter the temple until the seven plagues of the seven angels were finished.

Rev 16:1-21
CHAPTER 16

1	And I heard a loud voice from the temple, saying to the seven angels, "Go and pour out the seven bowls of the wrath of God into the earth."

2	And the first {angel} went and poured out his bowl into the earth; and it became a loathsome and malignant sore upon the men who had the mark of the beast and who worshiped his image.

3	And the second {angel} poured out his bowl into the sea, and it became blood like {that} of a dead man; and every living thing in the sea died.

4   And the third {angel} poured out his bowl into the rivers and the springs of waters; and they became blood.

5   And I heard the angel of the waters saying, "Righteous art Thou, who art and who wast, O Holy One, because Thou didst judge these things;

6   for they poured out the blood of saints and prophets, and Thou hast given them blood to drink. They deserve it."

7   And I heard the altar saying, "Yes, O Lord God, the Almighty, true and righteous are Thy judgments."

8   And the fourth {angel} poured out his bowl upon the sun; and it was given to it to scorch men with fire.

9   And men were scorched with fierce heat; and they blasphemed the name of God who has the power over these plagues; and they did not repent, so as to give Him glory.

10   And the fifth {angel} poured out his bowl upon the throne of the beast; and his kingdom became darkened; and they gnawed their tongues because of pain,

11   and they blasphemed the God of heaven because of their pains and their sores; and they did not repent of their deeds.

12   And the sixth {angel} poured out his bowl upon the great river, the Euphrates; and its water was dried up, that the way might be prepared for the kings from the east.

13   And I saw {coming} out of the mouth of the dragon and out of the mouth of the beast and out of the mouth of the false prophet, three unclean spirits like frogs;

14   for they are spirits of demons, performing signs, which go out to the kings of the whole world, to gather them together for the war of the great day of God, the Almighty.

15   ("Behold, I am coming like a thief. Blessed is the one who stays awake and keeps his garments, lest he walk about naked and men see his shame.")

16   And they gathered them together to the place which in Hebrew is called Har-Magedon.

17   And the seventh {angel} poured out his bowl upon the air; and a loud voice came out of the temple from the throne, saying, "It is done."

18　　And there were flashes of lightning and sounds and peals of thunder; and there was a great earthquake, such as there had not been since man came to be upon the earth, so great an earthquake {was it, and} so mighty.

19　　And the great city was split into three parts, and the cities of the nations fell. And Babylon the great was remembered before God, to give her the cup of the wine of His fierce wrath.

20　　And every island fled away, and the mountains were not found.

21　　And huge hailstones, about one hundred pounds each, came down from heaven upon men; and men blasphemed God because of the plague of the hail, because its plague was extremely severe.

Rev 19:1-21
CHAPTER 19

1　　After these things I heard, as it were, a loud voice of a great multitude in heaven, saying, "Hallelujah! Salvation and glory and power belong to our God;

2　　because His judgments are true and righteous; for He has judged the great harlot who was corrupting the earth with her immorality, and He has avenged the blood of His bond-servants on her."

3　　And a second time they said, "Hallelujah! Her smoke rises up forever and ever."

4　　And the twenty-four elders and the four living creatures fell down and worshiped God who sits on the throne saying, "Amen. Hallelujah!"

5　　And a voice came from the throne, saying, "Give praise to our God, all you His bond-servants, you who fear Him, the small and the great."

6　　And I heard, as it were, the voice of a great multitude and as the sound of many waters and as the sound of mighty peals of thunder, saying, "Hallelujah! For the Lord our God, the Almighty, reigns.

7   "Let us rejoice and be glad and give the glory to Him, for the marriage of the Lamb has come and His bride has made herself ready."

8   And it was given to her to clothe herself in fine linen, bright {and} clean; for the fine linen is the righteous acts of the saints.

9   And he said to me, "Write, 'Blessed are those who are invited to the marriage supper of the Lamb.'" And he said to me, "These are true words of God."

10   And I fell at his feet to worship him. And he said to me, "Do not do that; I am a fellow servant of yours and your brethren who hold the testimony of Jesus; worship God. For the testimony of Jesus is the spirit of prophecy."

11   And I saw heaven opened; and behold, a white horse, and He who sat upon it {is} called Faithful and True; and in righteousness He judges and wages war.

12   And His eyes {are} a flame of fire, and upon His head {are} many diadems; and He has a name written {upon Him} which no one knows except Himself.

13   And {He is} clothed with a robe dipped in blood; and His name is called The Word of God.

14   And the armies which are in heaven, clothed in fine linen, white {and} clean, were following Him on white horses.

15   And from His mouth comes a sharp sword, so that with it He may smite the nations; and He will rule them with a rod of iron; and He treads the wine press of the fierce wrath of God, the Almighty.

16   And on His robe and on His thigh He has a name written, "KING OF KINGS, AND LORD OF LORDS."

17   And I saw an angel standing in the sun; and he cried out with a loud voice, saying to all the birds which fly in midheaven, "Come, assemble for the great supper of God;

18   in order that you may eat the flesh of kings and the flesh of commanders and the flesh of mighty men and the flesh of horses and of those who sit on them and the flesh of all men, both free men and slaves, and small and great."

19   And I saw the beast and the kings of the earth and their armies, assembled to make war against Him who sat upon the horse, and against His army.

20   And the beast was seized, and with him the false prophet who performed the signs in his presence, by which he deceived those who had received the mark of the beast and those who worshiped his image; these two were thrown alive into the lake of fire which burns with brimstone.

21   And the rest were killed with the sword which came from the mouth of Him who sat upon the horse, and all the birds were filled with their flesh.

Rev 20:1-15
CHAPTER 20

1   And I saw an angel coming down from heaven, having the key of the abyss and a great chain in his hand.

2   And he laid hold of the dragon, the serpent of old, who is the devil and Satan, and bound him for a thousand years,

3   and threw him into the abyss, and shut {it} and sealed {it} over him, so that he should not deceive the nations any longer, until the thousand years were completed; after these things he must be released for a short time.

4   And I saw thrones, and they sat upon them, and judgment was given to them. And I {saw} the souls of those who had been beheaded because of the testimony of Jesus and because of the word of God, and those who had not worshiped the beast or his image, and had not received the mark upon their forehead and upon their hand; and they came to life and reigned with Christ for a thousand years.

5   The rest of the dead did not come to life until the thousand years were completed. This is the first resurrection.

6   Blessed and holy is the one who has a part in the first resurrection; over these the second death has no power, but they will be priests of God and of Christ and will reign with Him for a thousand years.

7   And when the thousand years are completed, Satan will be released from his prison,

8   and will come out to deceive the nations which are in the four corners of the earth, Gog and Magog, to gather them together for the war; the number of them is like the sand of the seashore.

9   And they came up on the broad plain of the earth and surrounded the camp of the saints and the beloved city, and fire came down from heaven and devoured them.

10   And the devil who deceived them was thrown into the lake of fire and brimstone, where the beast and the false prophet are also; and they will be tormented day and night forever and ever.

11   And I saw a great white throne and Him who sat upon it, from whose presence earth and heaven fled away, and no place was found for them.

12   And I saw the dead, the great and the small, standing before the throne, and books were opened; and another book was opened, which is {the book} of life; and the dead were judged from the things which were written in the books, according to their deeds.

13   And the sea gave up the dead which were in it, and death and Hades gave up the dead which were in them; and they were judged, every one {of them} according to their deeds.

14   And death and Hades were thrown into the lake of fire. This is the second death, the lake of fire.

15   And if anyone's name was not found written in the book of life, he was thrown into the lake of fire.

Rev 21:1-27
CHAPTER 21

1   And I saw a new heaven and a new earth; for the first heaven and the first earth passed away, and there is no longer {any} sea.

2   And I saw the holy city, new Jerusalem, coming down out of heaven from God, made ready as a bride adorned for her husband.

3   And I heard a loud voice from the throne, saying, "Behold, the tabernacle of God is among men, and He shall dwell among them, and they shall be His people, and God Himself shall be among them,

4   and He shall wipe away every tear from their eyes; and there shall no longer be {any} death; there shall no longer be {any} mourning, or crying, or pain; the first things have passed away."

5   And He who sits on the throne said, "Behold, I am making all things new." And He said, "Write, for these words are faithful and true."

6   And He said to me, "It is done. I am the Alpha and the Omega, the beginning and the end. I will give to the one who thirsts from the spring of the water of life without cost.

7   "He who overcomes shall inherit these things, and I will be his God and he will be My son.

8   "But for the cowardly and unbelieving and abominable and murderers and immoral persons and sorcerers and idolaters and all liars, their part {will be} in the lake that burns with fire and brimstone, which is the second death."

9   And one of the seven angels who had the seven bowls full of the seven last plagues, came and spoke with me, saying, "Come here, I shall show you the bride, the wife of the Lamb."

10   And he carried me away in the Spirit to a great and high mountain, and showed me the holy city, Jerusalem, coming down out of heaven from God,

11   having the glory of God. Her brilliance was like a very costly stone, as a stone of crystal-clear jasper.

12   It had a great and high wall, with twelve gates, and at the gates twelve angels; and names {were} written on them, which are {those} of the twelve tribes of the sons of Israel.

13   {There were} three gates on the east and three gates on the north and three gates on the south and three gates on the west.

14   And the wall of the city had twelve foundation stones, and on them {were} the twelve names of the twelve apostles of the Lamb.

15   And the one who spoke with me had a gold measuring rod to measure the city, and its gates and its wall.

16   And the city is laid out as a square, and its length is as great as the width; and he measured the city with the rod, fifteen hundred miles; its length and width and height are equal.

17   And he measured its wall, seventy-two yards, {according to} human measurements, which are {also} angelic {measurements.}

18   And the material of the wall was jasper; and the city was pure gold, like clear glass.

19   The foundation stones of the city wall were adorned with every kind of precious stone. The first foundation stone was jasper; the second, sapphire; the third, chalcedony; the fourth, emerald;

20   the fifth, sardonyx; the sixth, sardius; the seventh, chrysolite; the eighth, beryl; the ninth, topaz; the tenth, chrysoprase; the eleventh, jacinth; the twelfth, amethyst.

21   And the twelve gates were twelve pearls; each one of the gates was a single pearl. And the street of the city was pure gold, like transparent glass.

22   And I saw no temple in it, for the Lord God, the Almighty, and the Lamb, are its temple.

23   And the city has no need of the sun or of the moon to shine upon it, for the glory of God has illumined it, and its lamp {is} the Lamb.

24   And the nations shall walk by its light, and the kings of the earth shall bring their glory into it.

25   And in the daytime (for there shall be no night there) its gates shall never be closed;

26   and they shall bring the glory and the honor of the nations into it;

27   and nothing unclean and no one who practices abomination and lying, shall ever come into it, but only those whose names are written in the Lamb's book of life.

Rev 22:1-21
CHAPTER 22

1   And he showed me a river of the water of life, clear as crystal, coming from the throne of God and of the Lamb,

2   in the middle of its street. And on either side of the river was the tree of life, bearing twelve {kinds of} fruit, yielding its fruit every month; and the leaves of the tree were for the healing of the nations.

3   And there shall no longer be any curse; and the throne of God and of the Lamb shall be in it, and His bond-servants shall serve Him;

4   and they shall see His face, and His name {shall be} on their foreheads.

5   And there shall no longer be {any} night; and they shall not have need of the light of a lamp nor the light of the sun, because the Lord God shall illumine them; and they shall reign forever and ever.

6   And he said to me, "These words are faithful and true"; and the Lord, the God of the spirits of the prophets, sent His angel to show to His bond-servants the things which must shortly take place.

7   "And behold, I am coming quickly. Blessed is he who heeds the words of the prophecy of this book."

8   And I, John, am the one who heard and saw these things. And when I heard and saw, I fell down to worship at the feet of the angel who showed me these things.

9   And he said to me, "Do not do that; I am a fellow servant of yours and of your brethren the prophets and of those who heed the words of this book; worship God."

10   And he said to me, "Do not seal up the words of the prophecy of this book, for the time is near.

11   "Let the one who does wrong, still do wrong; and let the one who is filthy, still be filthy; and let the one who is righteous, still practice righteousness; and let the one who is holy, still keep himself holy."

12   "Behold, I am coming quickly, and My reward {is} with Me, to render to every man according to what he has done.

13   "I am the Alpha and the Omega, the first and the last, the beginning and the end."

14   Blessed are those who wash their robes, that they may have the right to the tree of life, and may enter by the gates into the city.

15   Outside are the dogs and the sorcerers and the immoral persons and the murderers and the idolaters, and everyone who loves and practices lying.

16   "I, Jesus, have sent My angel to testify to you these things for the churches. I am the root and the offspring of David, the bright morning star."

17   And the Spirit and the bride say, "Come." And let the one who hears say, "Come." And let the one who is thirsty come; let the one who wishes take the water of life without cost.

18   I testify to everyone who hears the words of the prophecy of this book: if anyone adds to them, God shall add to him the plagues which are written in this book;

19   and if anyone takes away from the words of the book of this prophecy, God shall take away his part from the tree of life and from the holy city, which are written in this book.

20   He who testifies to these things says, "Yes, I am coming quickly." Amen. Come, Lord Jesus.

21   The grace of the Lord Jesus be with all. Amen.